Praise for

"I gotta recommend this book, filled with history, wisdom, common sense, and laughs galore. I wish I had lived across the street from Charlie AND that I make it to 109!"

—Tom Hanks, on Instagram

"An original and highly readable account of a splendid American life."

—*The Wall Street Journal*

"As is true of Charlie himself, this book is not just about goodness but grit, not just kindness but courage. It is also a shining example of the magic that can happen when a master storyteller with a deeply inquiring mind finds a subject that has hidden within it a million tantalizing opportunities to learn, to question, and to grow. To say that *The Book of Charlie* is inspiring is a vast understatement. I am a better person for having read it."

—Candice Millard, author of *River of the Gods*

"No one writes as well about as many things as David Von Drehle, and his excellence is fully displayed in this slender examination of a well-lived life. In an era that elicits, by rewarding, incessant disparagement, he shows the beauty of elegant praise. You will never forget Charlie White, who was 102 when he came to Von Drehle's attention."

—George F. Will, syndicated columnist

"In every era, an author writes a genuinely original, formula-shattering book. David Von Drehle has done this in *The Book of Charlie*, a serious history of the last 100 years. *Charlie* is told through the personal story of one man, an accidental neighbor in Kansas, finding joy and what matters. I don't think it spoils the ending to divulge some of Charlie's lessons learned: 'Practice patience. Smile often. Savor special moments. Be soft sometimes.'"

—Bob Woodward

"There is something rather magical that David Von Drehle—one of our nation's most gifted chroniclers of history—met up with Charlie White, who lived longer than anyone you'll ever know. This Kansas City–set story is about goodness and the American spirit. It is also about time, and the graciousness in which a life can be lived on this green earth."

—Wil Haygood, *Colorization: 100 Years of Black Films in a White World*

"David Von Drehle's book is a monumental achievement cloaked in the experience of one ordinary American man of his time. In this stunningly true story, 100 years' worth of American eras become breathtakingly intimate experiences, history becomes personal, and a neighbor becomes a figure of deep nobility. You will never look at the folks next door the same way again."

—Sally Jenkins, author of *The Real All-Americans*

"A marvelous parable of resilience and durability, full of surprises and grace notes. David Von Drehle is among our most astute observers of the human condition, and in Dr. Charlie White—physician, centenarian, bon vivant—he has found a large character worthy of his talent."

—Rick Atkinson, author of *The British Are Coming*

"*The Book of Charlie* isn't just a loving look at an astonishing 110-year life, it's a look at ourselves."

—Rick Reilly, author of *Commander in Cheat*

"Excellent . . . Von Drehle gave his kids, kids in general, and people in general a how-to on life, and an important look back to the way life used to be. Hopefully it will alert them to how good they have it now. And is life ever good now. Read *The Book of Charlie* to see why."

—*Forbes*

"A splendidly woven, inspirational memoir that explores the meaning of life and the resilience of the human spirit. . . . This deeply engaging personal portrait of a remarkable centenarian also offers an absorbing account of the inventiveness of U.S. citizens—and the U.S., as it continually strives to evolve and improve."

—*Shelf Awareness*

"Von Drehle's detailed rendering of White's life—especially his front-seat view of (and sometimes participation in) groundbreaking medical developments—is fascinating, and the men's friendship affecting. This has a lot to offer."

—*Publishers Weekly*

The Book of Charlie

Wisdom from the Remarkable American Life of a 109-Year-Old Man

David Von Drehle

Simon & Schuster

New York   London   Toronto   Sydney   New Delhi

An Imprint of Simon & Schuster, LLC
1230 Avenue of the Americas
New York, NY 10020

First Simon & Schuster paperback edition May 2024

SIMON & SCHUSTER PAPERBACKS and colophon are registered trademarks of Simon & Schuster, Inc.

Simon & Schuster: Celebrating 100 Years of Publishing in 2024

For information about special discounts for bulk purchases, please contact Simon & Schuster Special Sales at 1-866-506-1949 or business@simonandschuster.com.

The Simon & Schuster Speakers Bureau can bring authors to your live event. For more information or to book an event, contact the Simon & Schuster Speakers Bureau at 1-866-248-3049 or visit our website at www.simonspeakers.com.

Interior design by Carly Loman

Manufactured in the United States of America

10 9 8 7 6 5 4 3 2 1

Library of Congress Cataloging-in-Publication Data is available.

ISBN 978-1-4767-7392-6
ISBN 978-1-4767-7393-3 (pbk)
ISBN 978-1-4767-7394-0 (ebook)

To Robert D. Richardson Jr.

Bob

1934–2020

Teacher, Captain, Friend

The Book
of Charlie

one

Nightly when my four children were young, I sat with a flashlight outside their bedrooms on the floor of the darkened hallway and read to them from chapter books. We read thousands of pages of Harry Potter and made hundreds of doughnuts with Homer Price. We spent time with Ramona and Beezus on Klickitat Street and sojourned in Narnia with the Pevensie children. We devoured diaries of a wimpy kid and reeled through volumes of unfortunate events. We thrilled to *The Red Badge of Courage* and wept over *Where the Red Fern Grows*. And of course, we returned more than once to the Arable farm, where miracles were woven into *Charlotte's Web*.

For many years, I enjoyed an audience of devoted listeners, but as the kids grew into their own concerns, I knew our shared time was coming to an end. They would soon have finals to study for, and crushes to FaceTime, and Netflix to stream deep into the night. The moment I was dreading arrived after we turned the last page of another adventure with Peter and the Starcatchers. My middle daughter suggested that we suspend our nightly reading indefinitely, and the others (more quickly than I would have hoped) chimed in to agree.

Sometime before we reached the end of our reading, the kids learned that Daddy was a writer of some kind, and they began asking me to write a book for them—the sort of book I could read aloud in the dark with my flashlight. I wanted very much to deliver for them, to pull a bit of magic from my hat and spin it into a tale both bracing and amusing, a story of brave and resourceful young people making their way in a marvelous and dangerous world. But every stab I took at writing a children's novel failed in one way or another. Gradually, I realized that my reading days would run out with their wish still unfulfilled, and that my failure to deliver a suitable story would be one more in a catalogue of ways in which I would disappoint them. A father hopes to be as extraordinary as his youngsters, in their innocence, imagine him to be, so that they need never become disillusioned with him. Perhaps some fathers accomplish that. As for me, my children matured, took notice of their father's shortcomings, and gave up asking for a book written just for them.

But now, here it is.

Admittedly, this is not the book they wanted. While there are plenty of exploits and perils and tragedies and amusements in the pages to come, none of them involve castles or pirate ships or even much tender romance. The main character has undeniable charms, but he's no hero, certainly no superhero. This book is bereft of wizards, crime-solving orphans, time travel, or empathetic talking spiders. It's not the book they asked for, but I believe it is a book they will need.

For this is a book about surviving, even thriving, through adversity and revolutionary change. Today's children—yours as well as mine—will live out their lives in a maelstrom of change. Some of it can be forecast. Other challenges will arrive as abruptly as a worldwide pandemic. I expect that self-driving cars and conversational robots are only the beginning, puffs of wind on the mild side of the storm. For cars and robots are gadgets, and gadgets evolve without necessarily changing the world. My own generation, after all, came of age with transistor radios and nineteen-inch Trinitrons. Now we have Spotify and eighty-five-inch UHD TVs. Yet we're still listening to music from handheld devices and watching two-dimensional pictures in motion behind a glass screen.

Revolutionary change is another matter. Revolutions have the power to remake societies and cultures and economies and political systems. Think of Gutenberg's printing press. Before print came along, there was no reason for most people to be literate. Information traveled slowly and unreliably by word of mouth or hand-copied manuscripts. Knowledge accrued very slowly because people knew only what they could learn from their elders in a family or village. The printing press made it possible for the first time to connect people cheaply and efficiently across broad distances and even across time. The follow-on effects were extraordinary: the Reformation, the Enlightenment, the scientific and industrial revolutions, the rise of democracy and free markets, the end of legal slavery, the age of exploration, including the exploration of space. All of these were made possible by print. If movable type—mere blocks of wood and slugs of lead—could do all that, what changes might be wrought through a revolution that places the world's libraries and languages in the palm of each hand and gives to every human being the power of mass communication?

The nature of work is changing, too, as more and more of the world's productivity derives from the interaction of humans and computers. History teaches that vast upheavals follow in the wake of workplace revolutions. When foraging gave way to farming, the world of tribes and nomads became a world of cities, states, nations, and empires. Cultures have been remade again wherever industrialization and market economies have replaced subsistence farming. The feudal world of kings and tsars became a mechanized world of finance and bureaucracy. For some, the new world was one of alienation and strife; for others, it was a world of freedom and aspirations. Women were liberated to have fewer children, for example. Having fewer children meant longer lives and time to think. The children they did have were better fed and endured less drudgery. Longer lives came to mean time for an education, and education taught people to dream. Today, we might suppose that parents have always hoped that their children would sail into brighter futures, but for most of human history, parents expected that their children would endure lives just as brutish and short as their own. Palace or hovel, one's birthplace was one's destiny.

I believe the digital revolution has already begun to spin off effects every bit as dramatic and vast as these past revolutions produced. Politics is being transformed by the disruptive power of social networks. Our news and information sources—the wellsprings of civic conversation—are unraveling under the power of infinite choice. Mating rituals are being recast by algorithmic yentas and virtual singles bars. Institutions are being undermined, while formerly localized threats, from terrorism to novel viruses, have gone global.

Parents want to give children the tools they need to succeed in life. But our kids are launching into a world so strange and unpredictable that a parent can't help but worry whether today's tool-kit might become tomorrow's burden. God forbid our advice takes them in the wrong directions.

As I've watched the growing magnitude of the digital revolu-tion, I've come to fear that I don't know enough about change to be of much help to my kids. I know about change at the gadget level, but have seen comparatively little of it at the levels of entire cultures and societies. Though I've marveled at many technological wonders through the years, my life has not been all that different from the lives of my parents. My mother and father grew up when radio was new, and I've lived to see radio splinter into broadcast, satellite, and wireless streaming. But my parents and I all lived in the time of radio. The same could be said of airplanes, newspapers, in-ternal combustion engines, network television, Republicans-versus-Democrats, "modern medicine," and a thousand more categories that have lent a stability to our lives even as the new gadgetry amazed us. During my children's lives, however, the categories themselves may be erased, and new categories created.

It dawned on me that I must go back another generation or two to find a role model and scout for them—a true surfer on a sea of change. I had to get back to the last years of the agrarian past, that moment when middle-class people lived without electricity or running water, when humans didn't fly and antibiotics didn't exist. I needed to find someone whose early life would have been recogniz-able to farmers from the age of Napoleon, or of Leonardo da Vinci. Someone from the world where horse-drawn carriages far outnum-bered automobiles, where pictures didn't move, and where kings ruled empires. An American born in the early 1900s who managed to live into the 2000s would have one foot planted in the age of draft animals and diphtheria—a time when only 6 percent of Americans graduated from high school—and the other planted in the age of space stations and robotic surgery. Such a person would have traveled from *The Birth of a Nation* to Barack Obama. From women forbidden to vote to women running nations and corporations. From Sunday potlucks in neighborhood churches to Sunday frenzies at football games where every big play is instantly rerun on screens five stories high. No human foot had ever touched the North or South Pole or the summit of Mount Everest when they were born, yet they lived to see footprints on the moon.

Children of the early 1900s who lived to a great age saw their lives and their communities, their places of work and of worship, their families and mores shaken, inverted, blown up, and remade. They entered the world at just the moment that (in the words of Henry Adams) history's "neck [was] broken by the sudden irruption of forces totally new," and they lived through the ever-changing consequences. What did it take to thrive and find happiness while experiencing so much disruption? Whatever it was, those were the tools I want to pass on to my children: the tools for resilience and equanimity through massive dislocation and uncertainty.

I decided to write a book for my children that would unlock the secrets of life inside the storm. And once I understood this was my task as their father, I would have gone to the ends of the Earth to find such a tale. But that proved unnecessary, because one blazing August morning I looked up from my driveway and saw my story standing there, just across the street.

two

The year was 2007. My wife and I had uprooted our children—ages nine, seven, six, and four—from Washington, D.C., to replant them in the suburbs of Kansas City, Missouri. As Karen once explained our decision, she had grown tired of the hassles of urban parenting: the traffic jams, long lines, and dollar-per-minute swim lessons. I had grown tired of people arguing with each other, which is the principal pastime of the nation's capital. I was starting a new job that allowed me to telecommute, and after many exciting years on the East Coast, this Colorado boy was ready to get back to the middle of the country, where the skies are bigger than the egos.

Our new home was still full of half-empty moving boxes on the morning in question. An August heat wave had settled over the Midwest, and though it was only 8 a.m., a wall of steamy oppression hit me when I stepped outside to fetch the Sunday newspaper, as if I'd opened a dishwasher too soon. Halfway down the driveway, I looked up, and through the glare of an already angry sun I saw something that stopped me in my tracks. My new neighbor was washing a car in his circular driveway across the street. In my memory (this detail is a matter of some disagreement around the neighborhood) the car he was washing was a shiny new Chrysler PT Cruiser, the color of grape soda pop. I like to believe that my memory is sharper than the recollections of those who say it was a less distinctive car. And my imagination is too dull to conjure a Fanta-colored automobile glittering in the neighbor's driveway. But if indeed I've dreamed up this aubergine buggy it can only be in tribute to the owner of the car, a woman of such charisma that ordinary wheels would not be worthy of her. (We'll meet her in due time, and she's worth the wait.)

This much is undisputed: my neighbor was, in the sunshine of an August Sunday morning, washing his girlfriend's car. I couldn't help but note that the vehicle in question was parked in the same spot where she had left it the night before. I deduced that his Saturday night date with the glamorous driver of the possibly purple car had developed into the sort of sleepover that makes a man feel like being especially nice the next morning.

My neighbor was bare-chested, dressed only in a pair of old swim trunks. With a garden hose in one hand and a soapy sponge in the other, he flexed his muscular chest with each splash and swirl, while his wavy hair flopped rakishly over one eye. This was Charlie White.

Age 102.

I had been introduced to the handsome doctor a few days earlier by his son-in-law Doug, who lived in the house next door to ours. Doug's wife at the time was Charlie's youngest daughter, and they had moved onto the street to keep an eye on her dad. Frankly, I didn't see the need. Charlie was hale and sturdy and razor-sharp. When we met, he offered what used to be known as a manly handshake—not a bone crusher, but a proper put-'er-there kind of squeeze, firm and sincere. His eyes were clear and sapphire blue. His hearing was good, and his conversation danced easily from topic to topic and from past to present to future and back. His flowing white hair and debonair mustache gave him an elegant, vaguely theatrical air—he reminded me a bit of Doc on *Gunsmoke*—amplified by the walking stick he held casually at his side. Even better, the walking stick proved on closer inspection to be a pitching wedge held upside down. Such casual stylishness, using a golf club as a cane, can only be pulled off if it comes naturally. A little trouble with his balance was keeping him off the golf course, Charlie told me ruefully that first day, but (here he waggled the inverted club) he expected to be back in the swing soon enough.

In summary, Charlie was an extraordinary specimen. Even so, one does not expect, upon meeting a man of 102, to be starting a long and rich friendship. Actuarial tables have no room for sentiment or wishes, and this is what they say: according to the Social Security Administration, in a random cohort of 100,000 men, only about 350—fewer than half of 1 percent—make it to 102. Among those hardy survivors, the average chap has less than two years remaining. After 104, the lives slip quickly away, like the last grains of sand in an hourglass.

Yet on this muggy Sunday morning, when Charlie looked up from his car washing and gave me a jaunty wave with his sponge hand, there was something about him that made me think his odds were not to be found on any chart or spreadsheet. Life seemed to rest more lightly on him than on other men. Though, as we shall see, he knew more than his share of sadness and hard work, Charlie didn't resent life's insults or protest its humiliations. Nor did he fail to enjoy its fleeting kindnesses and flashes of beauty, among which he now counted the rare chance to hand-wash a girlfriend's car shortly after his 102nd birthday, beneath the broad canopy of an old tree that was dying faster than he was, as everything—the car, the tree, the soapy sponge, the startled neighbor shuffling toward his newspaper, the slumbering girlfriend, and Charlie himself—spun swiftly through space aboard the miracle planet called Earth.

I would later hear a story about Charlie that seemed to represent this distinctive quality of grateful attention to the beauty of life, what the French call *joie de vivre*. It's a fleeting moment, nothing elaborate or abstruse, yet it points somehow to life's most liberating—and empowering—lesson. Maybelle Carter, matriarch of country-and-western music, strummed her Gibson guitar and sang forthrightly about keeping on the sunny side of life. The fourteenth-century mystic and visionary Dame Julian of Norwich survived the Black Plague to write with confidence that "all shall be well, and all manner of thing shall be well." The lesson, so simple yet so difficult, is that life can be savored even though it contains hardship, disappointment, loss, and even brutality. The choice to see its beauty is available to us at every moment.

The story involved Charlie and his beloved game of golf. Long after his peers at the Blue Hills Country Club had passed away, Charlie continued playing in the company of much younger men—men barely past eighty. One day, Charlie found himself standing on the green as his partner descended into a sand trap to play an errant ball. Sometime after the man disappeared from view into the deep bunker, Charlie saw a spray of sand along with his companion's ball, which hopped and rolled to a stop on the putting surface. Then . . . nothing. After some time passed, Charlie walked to the edge of the green and peered over to find the younger man struggling without success to climb out of the hazard. Charlie doubted his ability to pull the man out. What to do? Charlie's reaction was not concern or alarm. He didn't think: *What are we doing out here? We're too old for this.* He burst out laughing, and kept laughing until his friend was heaving with laughter, too. They were still laughing when the group behind them arrived to rescue the stranded octogenarian.

Charlie made an art of living. He understood, as great artists do, that every life is a mixture of comedy and tragedy, joy and sorrow, daring and fear. We choose the tenor of our lives from those clashing notes. Even when Charlie's strength was fading, when the golf course had become an obstacle course, when the infirmity of encroaching time could no longer be denied, he chose to turn his wedge into a walking stick and to carry it with panache.

Our arrival across the street from Charlie White turned out to be the start of a seven-year friendship. He defied the actuaries to become one of the last men standing—one of only five fellows from the original 100,000 expected to make it to 109. (Statistically speaking, only two make it to 110, and the last one winks out at around 111.) Charlie was among the last living Americans from the presidency of William Howard Taft, among the last surviving officers of World War II, among the last physicians who knew what it was to practice medicine before penicillin, among the last Americans who could say what it was like to drive an automobile before highways existed, among the last people who felt amazement when pictures moved on a screen, and sound emerged from a box. By the time Charlie was done, he lived nearly half the history of the United States. Born years before Walter P. Chrysler built his first car, Charlie was still around more than seven decades after Chrysler's death—enough years to see the soaring Chrysler Building age from a symbol of New York's glorious future into a totem of its past; enough years to find himself swabbing (as I remember it) a high-gloss purple roadster wearing the long-dead Chrysler's badge, a Chrysler equipped with remote keyless entry and an iPod jack.

Charlie was a man of science. As a physician, he knew how the human body goes—and how it stops. He was the first to say that his extraordinary life span was a fluke of genetics and fortune. Still, as I've reflected on this remarkable friend, I've come to see that he was more than a living history lesson, and more than just the winner of a genetic Powerball. He was a case study in how to thrive—not just survive, but thrive—through any span of years, short or long. People often asked him the secret of longevity, and Charlie was always scrupulously honest: there's no secret, just luck. But if he knew no secrets to a long life, he knew plenty about a happy life. Through tragedy and loss, poverty and setbacks, missteps and blown chances, he maintained a steadiness, an evenness, and a self-reliance that today might be called resilience. He had a gift for seizing joy, grabbing opportunities, and holding on to things that matter. And he had an unusual knack for an even more difficult task: letting go of all the rest.

His daughter Madelyn once told my wife a story that captures something essential to Charlie's personality. She had found herself enmeshed in some sort of neighborhood angst in which this person says something to that person who turns around and does something to somebody else, and can you *believe* anyone could do or say such things? Inevitably, Madelyn found herself on the receiving end of an irate phone call. Listening from the kitchen table, Charlie waited until she finally extricated herself. He waited some more while she described the situation. After a pause, he counseled his youngest to let it go. You'll kill yourself getting worked up, he told her. "I don't have time for people like that," he said.

The wisdom of centuries was packed into that laconic advice. Though Charlie was not a student of philosophy, I recognized in his words the essence of Stoicism, one of the most durable and useful schools of thought ever devised. It is a philosophy equally as compelling to an abused slave like Epictetus, the first-century Roman who smiled as his sadistic master twisted his leg until it snapped, as to the second-century Roman emperor Marcus Aurelius. The Stoics taught that a life well lived requires a deep understanding of what we control, and—more difficult—all that lies beyond our control. We determine nothing but our own actions and reactions. Our willful choices. A true education, Epictetus taught, consists of learning "to distinguish that among things, some are in our power but others are not; in our power, are will and all acts that depend on the will. Things *not* in our power are the body, the parts of the body, possessions, parents, brothers, children, country, and generally all with whom we live in society."

For the slave, this insight spoke to the determination of Epictetus to live with purpose and dignity even as a master controlled his body and actions. He could be bought and sold and worked like an animal, but he could not be made to think or act or *be* like an animal. "It is circumstances which show what men are," he taught his students after gaining his freedom. "Therefore, when a difficulty falls upon you, remember that God, like a trainer of wrestlers, has matched you with a rough young man . . . that you may become an Olympic conqueror; but it is not accomplished without sweat."

For the same reasons, Stoicism spoke to Viktor Frankl, an Austrian neurologist who survived the Nazi slave labor camps as a prisoner at

Dachau. From his observation of exemplary prisoners who maintained their dignity and goodwill even in those hellish circumstances, Frankl concluded that "everything can be taken from a man but one thing: the last of the human freedoms—to choose one's attitude in any given set of circumstances, to choose one's own way" of meeting whatever life presents. This same philosophy has spoken to generations of alcoholics seeking to be free of an enslaving addiction. "God grant me the serenity to accept the things I cannot change," their prayer goes, "courage to change the things I can; and wisdom to know the difference."

What Marcus Aurelius understood is that all of us are slaves in certain respects, even the emperor of Rome. We are slaves to time and chance; we are indentured to fate. "Love the hand that fate deals you and play it as your own," he wrote in his *Meditations*. In another gem, he observed that "it never ceases to amaze me: we all love ourselves more than other people, but care more about their opinion than our own."

Ralph Waldo Emerson arrived at the same wisdom: "A man is to carry himself in the presence of all opposition, as if every thing were titular and ephemeral but he." Rudyard Kipling praised those who "can meet with Triumph and Disaster / And treat those two impostors just the same."

"Let it go," counseled Charlie of the things beyond one's control. But Stoic self-possession is also the bedrock on which the qualities we now speak of as grit and resilience are built. Stoicism is the human fuel that gives us the greatest mileage. Kipling's famous poem goes on to praise the self-reliance that allows us to

> . . . *force your heart and nerve and sinew*
> *To serve your turn long after they are gone,*

And so hold on when there is nothing in you
Except the Will which says to them: "Hold on!"

Let it go and *Hold on!* In the way of so many great philosophies, those apparent opposites prove to be two sides of the same coin. To hold securely to the well-formed purposes of your own will, you must let go of the vain idea that you can control people or events or the tides of fate. You can't change what was, nor entirely control what will be. But you can choose who you are and what you stand for and what you will try to accomplish.

I've been learning and losing and relearning this lesson for some sixty years. But I think Charlie learned the essence of it in a single day and never forgot. He was a quick learner—and a prodigy, because he absorbed this wisdom, this elusive key to contentment in life, as a mere boy of eight. Remarkable.

But then, he had a heartless and harshly effective teacher.

three

Charlie was the third Charles Herbert White in his family tree, but the name did not mean much to him. "My mother just fell into that, I guess," he once said, "fell into the family tradition of naming sons after fathers." He was deeply proud of his connections to American history, though. Charlie traced his roots through his mother's line to Captain Thomas Graves, a Jamestown settler and member of the first legislative body in the colony of Virginia. Through his father's line, he connected with Virginia's aristocratic Carter family, which also settled at Jamestown. A century before the Declaration of Independence, Robert Carter was amassing such large holdings in land and enslaved labor, and wielding so much political power, that other Virginians nicknamed him "King." His descendants included two U.S. presidents and the Confederate general Robert E. Lee. Not to mention Charlie White, who felt a tingle of destiny about the convergence of bloodlines within him. "It's a strange thing, and unusual, that these two families, after about twenty generations, finally came together. That's about a one-in-a-billion chance," he mused. "You might say these two families are the original pioneers of America. I'm lucky to inherit that situation."

Born August 16, 1905, Charlie entered a world in which the Civil War was tangible. Veterans of the blood-soaked trauma of blue and gray were a part of daily life, their battles closer to Charlie than Vietnam is to a child born today. Though his first home was in Galesburg, Illinois—the Land of Lincoln—his Virginia lineage made him partial to the Rebs. Young Charlie idolized his grandfather on his father's side, the original Charles H. White, who had been a scout in the Confederate cavalry and retained his equestrian flair into his eighties. Charlie cherished visits to his grandparents' farm in Saline County, Missouri, where his grandmother told stories of hiding the family silver in cans of milk so the Yankees couldn't find it, while grandpa passed along his love of horses. Nearly a century later, Charlie still enjoyed telling of a surrey race, late in the old man's life, when the shaft broke on the buggy and the elderly horseman scrambled onto the trotter's back to finish the contest.

The boy inherited that spirit. He was a spunky kid. His first vivid memory, from age three or four, was of the streetcar that passed in front of his family's house, which sat at the end of the trolley line. Charlie and a neighbor boy loved to scamper up on the fender of the car as it slowly turned for another run. Sometimes they would try to hop inside for a joyride. The conductor demanded that Charlie's mother put an end to the dangerous game, but Laura White was too busy with the demands of her young family to supervise every passing streetcar. So she tied one end of a fifteen-foot rope to Charlie's ankle and lashed the other end to a tree. "I'm not going to watch you," he recalled her saying matter-of-factly. "I'm just going to hogtie you up here like I do the cattle."

Galesburg was a city of about twenty thousand people on the flatlands of America's Great Plains, a fertile vastness of grains and grasses dotted with farmhouses and pigsties, beribboned with dirt roads and wagon ruts, quieter by day and darker by night than most of us can now imagine. I suppose you would call it Small Town America, except that the distinction between small and large places was less definite in those days. The U.S. Census of 1900 found only six cities in the entire country with more than 500,000 residents. A population of 200,000 placed a city in the top 20 nationally; a population of 100,000 ranked in the top 40. Galesburg appeared to be moving smartly up the charts, a hive of commerce and ambition. There was nothing sleepy about the Midwest. The heartland states boomed with the business of feeding America and the world. Omaha, Nebraska, and St. Joseph, Missouri, were both more populous than Los Angeles or Atlanta or Seattle. Like Galesburg, which had grown nearly 400 percent in the previous four decades, Omaha and St. Joe were intersections in the fast-growing network of railroads that moved the travelers and freight of a rising nation. Galesburg's switching yards ran triple shifts to accommodate the trains of the Chicago, Burlington & Quincy line as they connected with the Atchison, Topeka & Santa Fe, dropping cars and picking up others in one of the most modern freight depots on Earth.

Charlie's father was a minister in the Christian Church (Disciples of Christ), an ecumenical denomination that sprang up in Kentucky, Tennessee, and western Pennsylvania in the early nineteenth century, during the nationwide revival known as the Second Great Awakening. The Disciples maintained that God was calling His children to unity, and sought to break down walls of doctrine that divided Protestants into bickering sects.

Raised on the family farm in Missouri, Charles H. White Jr. was a sturdy young man with curly hair and a widow's peak over a long nose. His parents sent him to the University of Kentucky, where the young scholar met a farm girl from the nearby town of Pinckard. He fell in love with Laura Graves, and after the newly ordained Rev. White set up shop at his first church, he married his twenty-year-old sweetheart in 1893.

The young pastor was easygoing and popular, with a quick sense of humor, his son would recall more than a century later. His preaching leaned toward clarity and straightforwardness rather than flights of poetry, and he struck themes that would echo years later in Charlie's philosophy. "We must forget past failures," he advised in one of his sermons, "for many times we forget the things of today in lamenting the failures of the past. . . . Some men regret the last rays of the setting sun, while others look toward the east for the first light of dawn."

However, the pulpit was not his strongest venue. His talent, he soon discovered, was managing the often-neglected business side of church life. "He was certainly adept at practical Christianity," as Charlie phrased it. The young pastor found himself moving frequently from one debt-burdened congregation to the next, stopping at each one just long enough to balance the books and restore the church's confidence. After lifting his first assignment, in Lebanon, Missouri, from a lake of red ink, Rev. White was called to a church in Joplin, westward along the trail that would become the famous highway Route 66. When the Joplin congregation was growing again and its finances were squared away, Rev. White headed next to Clarinda, Iowa, in the gently rolling countryside of the Missouri River valley.

Clarinda's flock of Disciples faced financial failure, but the fault might not have been entirely its own. The 1890s was a time of boom and bust in the American economy. And whenever Wall Street ran into another ditch, it seemed as though midwestern farmers paid the penalty. Their crop prices plunged, their mortgages were foreclosed on, their churches went bust. Many people felt the economy was rigged in favor of railroad magnates and financiers. Newspapers ran stories of Newport, Rhode Island, palaces with marble driveways, and in the very next column might show glimpses of hungry children in battered shacks or tenement slums. Some from among Rev. White's struggling congregation were likely swept into the tide of populism that took hold—a populism that was often anti-immigrant, closed-minded, and resentful of outside influences.

But the pastor preferred to swim in a different intellectual stream. In Clarinda, he accepted a prominent role in the local Chautauqua movement, the annual grassroots celebration of arts and ideas that spread across the heartland at the turn of the century. For people who had no radios or televisions or phonographs, people who lived hours away from the nearest library or theater, the summertime Chautauqua was a weeklong celebration of humanity and beauty distilled into long, languid days. Cities and towns joined the circuit to present Chautauqua festivals to picnicking families under prairie skies.

As a member of the Clarinda Chautauqua committee, Rev. White helped to select lecturers, acting troupes, musicians, and public figures from among the hundreds of performers who plied the Chautauqua trail. The Great Commoner, politician William Jennings Bryan, logged countless miles traveling from one campground to the next, touting his platform of fiscal and spiritual reform. Temple University founder Russell Conwell delivered his motivational speech

"Acres of Diamonds" more than six thousand times over some forty years. The Fisk Jubilee Singers introduced hundreds of white audiences to African-American spirituals, while reformer Maud Ballington Booth moved listeners to tears with her descriptions of life in America's prisons. One year, the Clarinda Chautauqua featured an address by the famous educator Booker T. Washington, founder of the Tuskegee Institute and author of *Up from Slavery*. Hundreds of Iowans crowded around a small platform to listen raptly as Washington spoke beneath towering shade trees.

In the spring of 1899, having brought the Clarinda church back from the brink, White moved with his family to Galesburg, where this "man of most pleasant personality"—as the local newspaper introduced him—threw himself into yet another rescue. By November, the pastor had already raised $3,750 to pay off debts and attracted seventy new members to his church. His family was growing, too; Charlie had three older sisters (and eventually another one younger).

So dawned the twentieth century in a world that had yet to see a human being fly; in a country where more than 75 million people owned a total of only 8,000 automobiles; where just 10 percent of doctors had a college education, and diarrhea was a leading cause of death. And yet, a feeling of unlimited possibility was spreading from the great cities of the world to reach places like Galesburg and Clarinda and Joplin. Some of White's churchgoers no doubt had ridden the train, a few years earlier, to the World's Columbian Exposition in Chicago, where Eadweard Muybridge projected the first motion pictures ever watched by paying customers, and George Ferris offered thrill rides on the huge iron wheel that bore his name. Some, too, must have read accounts of the Great Exposition of 1900 in Paris, where awestruck observers toured the Hall of Electrical Machines. Gigantic generators harnessed the power of lightning bolts while barely making a sound. In the lexicon of 1900, these machines were called "dynamos," a name that cuts straight to the excitement they stirred in observers who tried to imagine their implications. Such power could conquer night, regulate temperature, defeat drudgery, and someday (though that day was too far off for most to see) enable computers. It was there, in the presence of a dynamo in Paris, that Henry Adams declared—with equal parts wonder and worry—that the neck of history had been broken.

In this dawn, Charlie White entered the world to be doted on by his sisters and, for a little while anyway, tied to a tree in the yard by his mother. But that treatment was entirely uncharacteristic of Laura Graves White. In all of Charlie's other boyhood memories, he was the happy beneficiary of his mother's benign neglect. He was free to roam, explore, build fires and forts, play cowboys and Indians.

Just as he was preparing to start school for the first time, Charlie's world expanded when his father accepted a summons to lead a struggling church in a working-class neighborhood of Kansas City. The cost of raising five children had become a strain on a pastor's salary, and life in a larger city allowed him to supplement his earnings by working as a life insurance agent. The itinerant life of the serial church-rescuer had become a poor fit for a family man.

To a boy of four or five, Kansas City was a metropolis, populated by some 250,000 people, with nearly as many cows, pigs, sheep, and horses in the busy stockyards and stables of the West Bottoms. As the Whites approached the city by train, a prevailing breeze perhaps

wafted the pungent odor of Kansas City's prosperity into their car—
for in all the world only Chicago boasted more feedlots. Visitors
smelled the place before they saw it. Such names as Armour, Swift,
and Cudahy were emblazoned on the meatpacking factories that
loomed outside the windows as Charlie's train pulled into Union
Depot, a flood-damaged architectural mishmash. After collecting
the baggage, the White family passed into the bustling street. The
boy's ears filled with the bawling and braying of livestock and the
music from nearby taverns and brothels. The busy sights, the noise,
the stench of blood and dung: Kansas City overwhelmed the senses.
A different child might have been intimidated, but not Charlie. As his
family rode the vertical tramway that connected the train station to
the business district looming over the stockyards from a formidable
bluff, Charlie got his first eager look at the city he would call home
for more than a century.

Though the Whites were by no means wealthy, Rev. White's
industry and prudence paid off. In 1912, he was able to buy a
handsome new three-story house at the edge of one of the city's
wealthiest neighborhoods. A line of similar homes on tidy little
lots stood like soldiers along Campbell Street, each with the deep
front porch characteristic of prewar Kansas City. This enclave of
up-and-comers was just two blocks west of the imposing mansion
that housed William J. Smith, cable car magnate. A thirty-room pile
of Grand Canyon sandstone built in muscular Romanesque style, it
was the largest in a parade of homes along Troost Avenue known as
Millionaire's Row.

The mansions were impressive, but Charlie preferred to venture
in the opposite direction when school was out at Hyde Park Ele-
mentary. The new boy in town found a nearby hilltop from which

to observe the city's grandest construction project taking shape: a new train station to replace the one by the stockyards.

He liked to sit for hours and watch the colossal enterprise. Enclosing 850,000 square feet of floor space, Union Station would be the third-largest train terminal in the country at the time. Yet for all its ambition, the Beaux Arts behemoth was built with technologies little advanced from the days of Michelangelo. Men tugged at horses and mules as they dragged heavy scoops, while other men used picks and shovels to dig the vast pit for the foundation. Muscle power, human and animal, moved mountains of dirt, hoisted tons of stone, and poured acres of concrete. In heat and in cold for more than three years, the boy returned to the hillside again and again as the mighty edifice rose. The ceilings in the Great Hall soared ninety-five feet above the inlaid terrazzo floors. Chandeliers, each weighing nearly two tons, dangled in midair. Around Charlie's ninth birthday, the work was finally finished. Kansas City's new station opened to trains in late 1914 and quickly became one of the busiest railroad hubs in America.

But the boy on the hill was not only a watcher. School came easily for Charlie, so he had plenty of time for play. A new game called "basketball" was popular in Kansas City; in fact, the inventor of basketball, James Naismith, was coaching a fledgling team at nearby University of Kansas. Charlie and his friends nailed a fruit basket high on a wall to serve as a hoop and joined in the craze. They also enjoyed a brand of street hockey they called "shinny," played with sticks and a tin can.

They played with matches, too. One day, Charlie and his pals got a campfire going in the yard and Charlie decided to hop over it, back and forth, having heard that Indian braves did this as part of their war dances. He dressed for the part in fringed leggings, and as he jumped over the flames, the fringe caught fire. Fortunately, his mother was nearby and heard his frightened shouts. Laura White came running with a blanket and smothered the smoldering pants. From this close call, Charlie learned a lesson he was to apply some years later, when a Fourth of July sparkler set his young niece's dress aflame. He grabbed a rug from the porch and bundled her up, thus saving the girl from disfigurement or death.

If any part of Charlie's life during those first eight years was less than idyllic, he never mentioned it to me or to anyone else that I can find. In his memory, his was a larking early childhood. But whenever he recalled his boyhood, his memory would inevitably arrive at the day when so much changed in a matter of seconds. The day of Charlie's introduction to the carelessness of fate.

The year was 1914. Union Station was nearing completion. Europe and Asia still belonged to princes and pashas whose colonies were spread across the planet. May 11 dawned an ordinary spring day, the day Charlie's baby sister was turning five. It was a Monday, when Rev. White took off his pastoral robes and donned the garb of the life insurance agent. After breakfast, the senior White left the house on Campbell Street and headed downtown. He probably took a streetcar, though he could have hailed a horse-drawn taxi.

Charlie's father was old enough to remember when the tallest thing in most cities was a steeple or a grain elevator. But now he occupied an office on the ninth floor of a twelve-story skyscraper in the heart of downtown Kansas City. This high-rise wonder was the fruit of two convergent technologies: steel bridgework and the electric passenger elevator. The skeleton of a steel-girder hotel or office tower was, in a sense, a trestle bridge turned on one end. As railroad bridges had shown, these relatively light frames could carry very heavy loads, so the sky was now the limit. Towers sprouted in cities across the country. By one count, three new high-rises of ten stories or more topped out in New York City every two weeks between 1900 and 1910. No doubt, the White family had read about the recent opening of the new record holder as the world's tallest tower: the Woolworth Building in New York soared nearly eight hundred feet above lower Broadway.

Kansas City's Gloyd Building, which housed White's office, was no threat to that record, but still it loomed 178 feet above Walnut Street. Completed in 1909, it stood in the shadow of the nearby National Bank of Commerce Building, part of a burgeoning skyline announcing that this cow town was now a boomtown. Along with its scale, the Gloyd Building boasted of its safety. As the city's first tower built of reinforced concrete, it was billed as "absolutely fireproof."

Around 10 a.m., Charlie's father rose from his desk, donned his coat and hat, lit his pipe, and left his office on a business errand. He planned to walk to the nearby City Market to collect the premium on a client's life insurance policy. When he reached the elevator in the corridor, he might have noticed that the usual operator was not at the controls. The door was open. A substitute stood with his hand on the lever.

As Rev. White moved into the car, the operator unexpectedly put the elevator in motion, lurching upward, the doors still open. This created an empty space between the unmoving floor of the hallway and the rising floor of the elevator, which was now waist-high. It happened so quickly that instead of stepping into the car, White's foot found the open space beneath.

His upper body pitched onto the floor of the rising car, his legs dangling in the abyss of the shaft. In an instant, the climbing car crushed the pastor's torso against the upper door frame so violently that the impact left a dent. Horrified by the sight of the man sandwiched half in and half out of his car, the inexperienced operator panicked and threw the elevator into reverse. But when the compartment lurched downward, White's upper body slipped free and followed his feet into the shaft. Charlie's father plunged nine stories to his death, his body bouncing from wall to wall as he fell. He was forty-two years old. His pipe and hat were found on the floor of the car.

I heard Charlie tell this story at least half a dozen times, and not once did he indulge in the sort of "Why, God?" questions that so naturally follow a freak accident. He never remarked on the apparent injustice of this good man's premature death in a world where history's most murderous despots—men such as Hitler, Stalin, and Mao—had decades of life left ahead of them. Charlie had no time for what-ifs: What if an experienced operator had been at the elevator controls? What if Rev. White had set out on his errand five minutes earlier or five minutes later? What if he had forgotten his tobacco and turned back toward his office? For Charlie, what happened, happened. It was over and he could do nothing to change it.

But that composure was hard earned. Immediately after the tragedy, Charlie's grief was so great that he could hardly eat. Charlie's mother and older sisters worried that he might starve. The whole family was overwhelmed. "My mother was devastated," Charlie recalled. In one fluky moment, she was left alone with five children and no income.

Over the years of our friendship, I spent hours listening to Charlie tell stories from his life. With time, I noticed a tone shift after his father's death. The spunky boy who had to be tied to a tree still made occasional appearances in Charlie's narration. But now he wore an armor of self-reliance. Just eight years old, Charlie became as independent as Huckleberry Finn, as resourceful as the Artful Dodger. As I reflected on this subtle key change, it occurred to me that after suffering a loss so enormous, and surviving it, Charlie decided he could get through anything. Brought face-to-face with the limits of his ability—of anyone's ability—to master fate or turn back time, Charlie began reaching for the things he could control: his own actions, his own emotions, his own outlook, his own grit.

four

As a grief-stricken boy in Kansas City was pushing his uneaten dinners around his plate, while his stunned and fearful mother wondered how she would hold her family together after her husband's shocking death, far away in Vienna, Austria, a doctor named Sigmund Freud was wrestling with questions of loss and trauma. Why was it that some people become trapped by traumatic events, mired in mourning, reliving their pain over and over again through obsessions, or nightmares, or what were then known as "hysterical" reactions?

This was before Freud was a global celebrity. Indeed, the pioneering neurologist was at a low point in his career, following his dramatic split with his acolyte Carl Jung. Freud feared that psycho analysis, his bold contribution to understanding the human mind, might fizzle out. His book on the function and meaning of dreams had been a sensation in certain intellectual circles. But no more than a handful of Kansas City residents would have known his name. A cigar was still just a cigar in 1914. Freud's scandalous, creative, insightful (and often misguided) guesswork about human psychology was a fuse lit—but the bomb had not yet detonated. When it did explode, it would knock the pillars out from under Victorian repression and license the sexual candor of the twentieth century.

But for now, Freud was dissatisfied. His idea of the human psyche was rooted in his theory of a life force, a compulsion to live and love. The life force, or libido, expressed itself in different attachments at different stages of development, but always it pursued life and pleasure. Freud identified this force with the Greek god Eros. However, as his radical reputation grew, and more patients found their way to Freud's Turkish-carpet-covered chaise for analysis, he was coming to the reluctant conclusion that his erotic framework was too simple. The grip of trauma and grief in some patients seemed to be the opposite of a life force. Freud could not explain it in terms of a "pleasure principle," as he had called his earlier notion.

Freud's database of trauma was about to swell dramatically, for three months after the death of Rev. White, Europe plunged heedlessly into a continental conflagration that would leave millions dead and wounded. That terrible world war left Freud, like the rest of his intellectual generation, deeply shaken and disillusioned. It "destroyed not only the beauty of the countrysides through which it passed and the works of art which it met with on its path," he later wrote, "but it also shattered our pride in the achievements of our civilization, our admiration for many philosophers and artists, and our hopes of a final triumph over the differences between nations and races. It tarnished the lofty impartiality of our science, it revealed our instincts in all their nakedness, and let loose the evil spirits within us which we thought had been tamed forever by centuries of continuous education by the noblest minds."

This catastrophe led Freud to conclude that another force—

a force his disciples associated with the god Thanatos—is also at work in the human mind, ensnaring a wounded psyche in mourning, sorrow, and death. Eros and Thanatos. Life and death. Being and nonbeing. Freud's observations sparked a revolution in psychology to match the revolutions in literature, art, music, and society that erupted from the so-called Great War. Long after his couch became a cultural cliché, generations of Freud's successors zeroed in on the lasting effects of psychic damage. Through a century of unprecedented violence and dislocation—the Great War giving way to the Russian Revolution and the Armenian genocide, followed by the Great Depression, the communist purges, the starving of Ukraine, and the Rape of Nanjing; bleeding into World War II, the Holocaust, and violent struggles for colonial independence—there was never a shortage of trauma for doctors to study.

Ideas of "hysteria" and "shell shock," current during Charlie's childhood, were shaped and reshaped over this century of pain into today's diagnosis: post-traumatic stress disorder (PTSD). Symptoms of this psychic damage can be deadly: homicides, suicides, and fatal accidents have all been linked to PTSD. An estimated 10 percent of all women and 5 percent of all men experience it at some point in their lives, according to an estimate from 2014—the year Charlie died, and a century after Charlie's father went to work one May Monday and never came home.

Only toward the end of that century did doctors begin to probe deeply for the boundaries and limits of Thanatos, asking how and why some people escape its trap. What characteristics allow some to experience trauma without being undone or diminished by it? Earlier, I quoted the great Stoic of the Holocaust, Viktor Frankl, whose book *Man's Search for Meaning* explored precisely this question under the most horrible of conditions. A Viennese psychiatrist following in the footsteps of Freud, Frankl survived more than two and a half years in Nazi concentration camps thanks to his usefulness as a doctor. During that time, he observed ghastly stress and trauma, and he found himself transfixed by those prisoners who somehow retained, even magnified, kindness, integrity, and dignity amid the inhumanity. Eventually he concluded that even in the worst pain, humans can choose to infuse meaning into their experiences, saying, "what is to give light must endure burning."

In recent decades, psychologists caring for trauma survivors have built on such work, and not long ago, the American Psychological Association distilled their findings into a straightforward recipe for "resilience" under stress. Reading through the traits and strategies of resilient people, I found myself face-to-face with young Charlie White.

The APA counsels trauma survivors to "take decisive actions"; these need not be world changing or even consequential, but they must be affirmative. Decisive action reflects our power over our wills even when we lack power over our circumstances. Frankl described a forced march in bitter cold to perform slave labor at Dachau; in his misery he directed his thoughts to his love for his wife. In a flash of transcendence, "I understood how a man who has nothing left in this world still may know bliss, be it only for a brief moment," he wrote. Frankl's choice of thoughts was the only "decisive action" available to him in that awful circumstance, and it proved his determination to fight free of Thanatos by asserting the life force. In the grip of depression or anxiety, any affirmative step is better than paralysis. Action promotes more action; decision produces decision; living generates life.

When we pick up Charlie's story in the dazed aftermath of his father's violent death, we see that something in this boy already grasped the existential truth. Though a child controls little, Charlie asserted himself as he could. He announced one day to his mother and sisters that he was going to sleep outside every night for a year. And just as impressive: his mother said yes. "You know, kids get ideas," Charlie said years later as he recounted the story. "But the thing was, my mother would let me carry them out." As he told it, Charlie put up a cot on a porch of the house on Campbell Street and slept there nightly, through the humid cloak of late July and the bitter chill of January. "I remember those cold, frigid mornings," he said. "Mother let me do it, see, that was the thing."

Laura White cultivated her son's confidence in ways large and small. "You are the man of the house now," he remembered her saying after his father died. She assigned him duties and responsibilities, starting with the care of their little yard and expanding—when he was strong enough—to managing the household coal supply. "They dumped the coal in the street," a mountain of coal to a boy, a full ton. "It was my job to take a wheelbarrow, and move the coal to the basement window and pour it into a coal bin. Then I had to keep the coal fire burning," Charlie recalled. "In the mornings, about four o'clock, I'd get up and pull the clinkers out and put fresh coal in to start the fire. Mother put the responsibility of life on me at an early age."

This might have backfired with another child, but Charlie found his mother's confidence liberating. Being treated as a survivor helped him to survive. With his father gone, he embraced the idea that "it was time to grow up." He saw this as an opportunity rather than a burden.

In this way, too, he was a model of the APA's resiliency traits. "Developing confidence in your ability to solve problems and trusting your instincts helps build resilience," the psychologists advise. Or as Charlie put it in recalling his childhood: "There were no restraints, really. You succeeded or failed by your own ability." His mother "guided us by not guiding. She guided by putting us on our own responsibility."

Laura White also taught her son by example. She was an intelligent woman, "strong and opinionated," her son said. "You knew where she stood. And you knew that her principles were of the highest quality." Acting decisively, with self-reliance and self-confidence, she quickly found a job managing mission trips for a religious organization, and supplemented her earnings by taking in boarders. Working two jobs, she managed to make ends meet.

For years Charlie and his sisters dined alongside the single men who paid for bed and board in the spare rooms of the Campbell Street house. Meals were served "family style" from Laura White's repertoire of southern recipes. (Charlie was partial to her beaten biscuits and spoon corn bread.) As he chewed, the boy studied these men as possible versions of his own irrepressible future. He judged them to be "high quality" men, as he put it. "I was exposed at the dinner table to guys like George Mansfield," circulation manager of the local newspaper, and Jack Noonan, an electrician who would marry one of Charlie's sisters. He found himself especially drawn to the missionaries who came to Campbell Street through his mother's work with the church. These men were intrepid, world travelers, healers. At that table, among such exemplars, Charlie told me, he first pictured himself as a doctor.

But that's getting ahead of the story. Our topic now is trauma and resiliency. And before we visited Freud in Vienna we had the picture of a grieving boy, suddenly fatherless, refusing to eat all but a very few foods. School had just ended for the summer. The spirited table talk of visiting missionaries lay unknown in the future; the mood at home was dismal. "With all the depression and all," as Charlie remembered this low point, "my mother thought it best if I get out of the influence of all of the girls." Laura White and her daughters tried to comfort Charlie, but maybe what the boy needed was the very thing he had lost: a male influence. Charlie's mother decided to send him to summer camp.

The idea of organizing forays in the wilderness for city boys (and later girls) was another manifestation of the enormous changes sweeping society. Industrialization and urbanization were seen as twin threats to burgeoning manhood. Victorian philosopher John Stuart Mill posited a direct link between the march of progress and the death of heroism. "A natural consequence of the progress of civilization," he wrote, is "moral effeminacy, [and] an inaptitude for every kind of struggle." Psychologist G. Stanley Hall, in his influential 1904 book, *Adolescence,* promoted the idea that children must start out wild before maturing into domesticity. City life interrupted that development by breaking boys' spirits. "A boy is not a sitting-down animal," preached Robert Baden-Powell, founder of the Boy Scouts, who staged his first camp in 1907, "The open-air is the real objective of Scouting and the key to its success."

By one scholar's count, the number of summer camps in the United States grew more than tenfold during Charlie's boyhood, from fewer than 100 at the turn of the century to more than 1,000 in 1918. The camp Charlie's mother stumbled upon was called the Boy Crusaders, near the Ozark Mountains hamlet of Anderson, Mis-

souri, in the extreme southwest corner of the state. As Charlie recalled nearly a century later, the camp's proprietor—and apparently
the only staff member—was an unmarried osteopath whose family
ran a prosperous clinic near Kansas City specializing in nonsurgical
treatment of hemorrhoids. Boy Crusaders was designed for adoles-
cent boys, but Laura White's urgent need for help with her grieving
son earned Charlie a last-minute enrollment. On the day appointed
for camp to begin, the soon-to-be third grader boarded a train in
the company of a dozen or so older boys, most in their teens, for the
trip to Anderson and a month in the mountains.

When they arrived at the spartan campsite, Charlie discovered
that Boy Crusaders took the back-to-nature gospel to extremes. "As
soon as we got down there, he took all of our clothes," Charlie recounted of the camp leader. "He said, 'You have to take your clothes
off.' We ran around for a month like natives without any clothes.
Oh, we were happy! We lived just like Indians, you know. We lived a
real rugged life." Apparently, the osteopath wasn't much for preparation. When the camp ran out of milk, he instructed a couple of
the boys to get dressed and hike to a nearby farm to buy some. Most
meals were simple oatmeal, Charlie said—a diet that cured him
completely of his cranky dining habits. "When I came home I was
like an aborigine: I'd eat anything."

Attitudes about nudity were different in those days. Boys' Clubs,
YMCAs, and even public high schools actually required boys to swim
naked, on the theory that it was more sanitary than swimming in
primitive bathing suits. But a month in the nude was abnormal even
then, and over the years of our friendship, as I listened to Charlie's
stories again and again, I began to suspect that he was leaving something out of his camp narrative. Something traumatic.

Here's what he did say. After sketching his improbable stay at "the craziest camp you could imagine," Charlie sometimes added matter-of-factly that Boy Crusaders did not last more than a few years after that summer, because complaints were lodged that the naked campers were being sexually molested. According to Charlie, when authorities followed up on these complaints, the osteopath's influential family pulled strings to hush up the scandal while dispatching their son to live in Europe. I've tried and failed to find any record of the camp or of the scandal, but I did confirm that the doctor in question left Kansas City to spend many years in Europe. He studied art, became an accomplished watercolorist, and joined several exclusive London clubs. By 1940, he was living in Paris, where he experienced life under Nazi occupation. Only after World War II did he return to the United States, where he delivered lectures about the Nazis to Chautauqua audiences and Rotary clubs. Charlie occasionally read his art reviews in the *Kansas City Star*.

Boy Crusaders was not a large camp. As I understood Charlie's stories, the boys on the train from Kansas City may have been the entire contingent. Yet despite the close quarters, Charlie always insisted that the abuse didn't affect him. "I was so young I wasn't exposed to that," he said. I believed him, as far as that went; a sexual predator attracted to teenagers might well leave a younger child alone. But something about Charlie's cheerful account nagged at me, and my doubts snapped into place as I listened to an interview he recorded not long after his one hundredth birthday. In three sessions of an hour each, he taped an oral history, and his family shared these recordings with me after he was gone.

A line jumped out as I listened: "I remember I really became tough down there," Charlie said of the camp. That adjective—*tough*—was out of sync with the rest of the story, which he always told with a chuckle and a sense of frolic. Maybe he was simply referring back to his statement that the boys "lived a real rugged life" at camp. But Sigmund Freud might ask whether that word was a telltale sign of something repressed. Charlie was an eight-year-old boy in the midst of preyed-upon naked teenagers. The fact is well documented that victims of sexual abuse often become offenders, and older boys bullying younger ones is a familiar, if lamentable, pattern. When Charlie said, "I was so young I wasn't exposed to that," he was speaking of the doctor's alleged molestations. But it occurred to me that, in such an atmosphere, Charlie might have been targeted by an older boy, or boys. And that might be why he became so tough that summer.

My suspicion that Charlie was somehow traumatized at camp led me to see another part of this story through different eyes. When telling his tale of the crazy camp, Charlie typically ended with an anecdote about the trip home. He said he was so eager to get back that he hopped from the slow local train when it stopped in Martin City, some twenty miles south of downtown Kansas City, and walked alone to the nearest streetcar. The first couple of times I heard this, I was charmed by the brave little scamp navigating the farmland and scattered settlements to find his way home. But the more I thought about it, the less sense it made. Even allowing for a sweeping turn around downtown to reach the old depot near the stockyards, surely the train wasn't slower than a walking boy. Nor was he, at eight, an experienced traveler who knew all the shortcuts. Charlie had some experience traveling by train to his grandparents' farm, but that trip covered different ground than the route to camp and back.

Did he leave the train because he was impatient to get home—or because he was eager to get away from his fellow campers? If Charlie was bullied or bothered by older boys, he would have ample reason to leave them at the earliest practical opportunity.

Whatever his motivation for striking out on his own, when he finally arrived home, Charlie's mother didn't immediately recognize him. A month spent naked in the sun had left him brown as an acorn. Laura White asked about her son's camp experience. He gave the same cheerful report he would give for the rest of his life—whether or not it was entirely true. Charlie was determined not to add to his mother's burdens. "I had so much respect for my mother, I would never bring any more problems into her thoughts," he later explained. The best way to protect her, he figured, was to refuse to turn his experiences, good or bad, into baggage. Live, learn, and move on. And so the salient fact of Charlie's camp story may ultimately be that—whatever happened in that place where "oh, we were happy"—Charlie never went back.

Sometime after Charlie's death, I shared my nagging questions about the Boy Crusaders with his son-in-law, my friend and neighbor Doug. A talented courtroom litigator, Doug has built a distinguished career on his ability to poke holes in stories that don't entirely add up. It turned out that he harbored his own doubts about Charlie's camp narrative; something was missing, he sensed.

He added some circumstantial evidence of his own: In the winter of 2012, Doug remembered, he was often with Charlie while reports of a sex abuse scandal at Penn State University dominated the news. The career of legendary football coach Joe Paterno came to an ignominious end amid revelations that a longtime assistant, Jerry Sandusky, was known to wrestle, shower, and travel in the company of underage, vulnerable boys. University officials, including Paterno, failed to act on a report of sexual assault by Sandusky. Eventually a Pennsylvania jury found Sandusky guilty of more than forty counts related to molestation of multiple victims. To Doug's surprise, Charlie minimized the severity of the matter.

We speculated that if Charlie had chosen, as a young boy, to minimize a traumatic experience at camp, he might feel compelled years later to downplay the damage caused by similar experiences of others. I think of the way my father typically reacted to the bruises, concussions, and broken bones of his children. He assured us that he had been through similar pain and come out just fine. "Shake it off," he'd say. This approach might make one appear callous to the suffering of others, but it is also a strategy for building endurance and fostering hope. "Cultivating the ability to leave traumatic events behind" is another of the APA's tools for resilience, and one way of doing so is to minimize their power to do lasting harm.

Even as a boy, Charlie saw no alternative to pressing ahead. "I don't remember being awfully happy," he once said of his boyhood, but he chose not to dwell on unhappiness. As he put it, "We didn't have time to be sad." In this attitude, Charlie manifested a precocious Stoicism. He would not be a slave to the actions, decisions, fates, or offenses of others. He anticipated the advice of author Leo Buscaglia, who urged: "Why do you cling to pain? There is nothing you can do about the wrongs of yesterday." Or as the APA frames the matter: resilient people choose to "avoid seeing crises as insurmountable problems." Instead they view trauma as a painful chance to grow stronger. Remember Epictetus: misfortune is the hard training that shapes our inner Olympians.

Still, Charlie was only a boy, and it would be wrong to suggest that his heart didn't break from time to time. When his elderly self looked back on those days, moments of loneliness stung more sharply than moments of trauma. He remembered vividly the pain that would wash over him when he noticed a boy of roughly his own age, and the boy was with a father—a vital, breathing, present father. They were laughing or having lunch or playing catch together. These were the hardest times, Charlie said, when loss slapped him in the face, and sadness dragged him down. Only with time, as the months turned to years, did Charlie learn to trust that these dark waves of depression would pass.

Once he learned, though, he never forgot. This knowledge was a resource he would tap through a lifetime of setbacks and losses. "Hardships aren't taken the same way by all people," he said. Indeed, some people are trapped by hardship; others use adversity to assert their truest freedom.

Charlie had a way of making everything sound like fun, even his mandatory weekly attendance at Linwood Christian Church. Evidently, Laura White got her fill of Sunday services during her tenure as a pastor's wife, because she dispatched Charlie while she remained at home. "She said, 'You go to church,' but she didn't go with me," he recalled. This was "unusual," Charlie allowed, but also reflected his growing independence.

Charlie liked church well enough. The often dreary Bible studies led by the dutiful woman who taught Sunday school were brightened by tales of frontier outlaws and pioneer perils spun by the woman's husband, a detective on the city police force. Charlie also approved of the preacher, who "gave a wonderful sermon," in his opinion. The boy tackled churchgoing with the same doggedness he applied to sleeping outdoors, and was rewarded with a pin after seven years of attendance without missing a single Sunday.

During the week, he attended grade school in Hyde Park, a prosperous neighborhood in walking distance of home. Though he "was just an average student" by his own reckoning, his teachers evidently disagreed. Especially after his father's death and the summer at camp, they saw in Charlie a maturity missing from his classmates. Midway through his third-grade year, they switched him into fourth grade, and the following year they advanced him again, from fifth grade to sixth. Two years younger than his peers when he started high school, Charlie nevertheless blended easily and eagerly into the social scene at Westport High.

America was in the midst of an accelerating transition from a society in which education belonged to the few to a society in which it was a universal right and expectation—at least for white children like Charlie. Segregated Westport High was emblematic of that change. The imposing red-brick edifice opened in 1908, at a time when only about 10 percent of Americans ages 14 to 17 enrolled in school. By the time Charlie entered ninth grade in 1917, that 10 percent share had roughly tripled. (A generation later it would be around 70 percent.)

As high school became more inclusive (in some ways), educators worried about the parallel rise of exclusive high school fraternities and sororities. In essays and frequent panel discussions, leading principals and school superintendents blamed these often snobbish groups for all sorts of vice and division among students. A 1904 report by Chicago school authorities, for example, charged that "the effect of secret societies is to divide the school into cliques, to destroy unity and harmony of action and sentiment, and to render it more difficult to sustain the helpful relations which should exist between pupils and teachers."

Charlie couldn't disagree more. "High school fraternities were great things in those days," he said fondly of the pack of boys who initiated him into their fellowship at Westport. His fraternity, called Delta Omicron Omicron, had its own honor code, which was enforced at regular sessions of a tribunal composed of the older members. "You had a kangaroo court at every meeting," Charlie recalled. "If one of the young guys was acting out of line, he had to stand up before the criticism of the boys." He remembered errant friends reduced to tears by the experience, yet he remained convinced throughout his life that this exercise in accountability "was one of the great influences anybody could have had. There's nothing like the criticism of your peers. We got that early in life, in high school."

For fun, the boys took the streetcar to Electric City, a wonderland of twinkling lights, gushing fountains, and thrill rides at the south end of town. They scavenged lost golf balls at a local course and taught themselves the game. They gathered on Main Street near school and roamed as a gang from one girl's house to another. "We might make half a dozen calls" in one Sunday afternoon, he said. Parents weren't altogether happy to see them coming, because the boys "all smoked" and dropped their cigarette butts into the cuffs of their trousers. But as Charlie noted, many of the swaggering young men went on to successful careers as lawyers, judges, doctors, and businessmen. One of Charlie's closest fraternity friends, Charles Parker, sailed for Oxford University as a Rhodes scholar in 1927.

All the while, work was as much a part of his life as school and friends. Charlie cut grass for his neighbors. He toiled in nearby farm fields during the harvest season. At sixteen, he took a job as an apprentice with his brother-in-law Jack Noonan, the electrician. Every day after school was out, Charlie showed up at Noonan's chandelier store downtown. "They'd give me a load of fixtures to hang, and they'd give me one of their cars. I'd go out and hang a whole house full of fixtures in an afternoon," he remembered. Many homes were switching from gaslight to electricity, so the young apprentice learned to disconnect the volatile gas lines and wire the sparking electric lights. Somehow he managed not to burn any houses down.

When he graduated from high school that year, Charlie White felt tested by adversity and seasoned by success. He was the friend and equal of older classmates. He was a help to his mother and a contributor to his family's finances. He had been pushed to grow up quickly by his father's untimely death, but doing so had fostered a quiet confidence in his own capacity. He had shown himself to be resourceful, responsible, self-disciplined, and resilient.

In this mood and moment, Charlie launched himself on a journey few people had ever taken before, a voyage into the future, a quest, an epic joyride.

five

Not long after the morning when I spotted Charlie washing his girl-friend's car, I was outside with the kids. Charlie stepped from his front door, hollered, and waved. He had something to show us. We followed him through the gate at the side of his house and into his backyard. In the far corner stood a playhouse, built to match his spacious home, and painted the identical mossy shade. Worn and cobwebbed after years of disuse, the playhouse nevertheless struck the kids as rich with potential. "Use it anytime," Charlie told them.

He led us back through the gate and into his house. There, in the front room, stood a life-sized figure of Santa Claus (though it was mid-August). "Wait till you see this!" Charlie said with glittering eyes. His balance issues were nowhere in evidence as he stooped nimbly to grab an electrical cord and, with only the slightest fumbling, sank the plug into the wall socket. Instantly Santa's eyes lit up, his head cocked and his weight shifted. "Ho, ho, ho!" came the familiar voice. With gesturing arms and a mouth that moved, the animatronic Kris Kringle sang a few lines of a Christmas carol.

The kids shot looks my way, unsure what to make of this. A singing Santa five and a half feet tall was exciting, to be sure. But why was he here in an old man's living room during the dog days of summer? Charlie explained that Santa was a gift from one of his daughters; he found the jolly fellow amusing and saw no reason to pack him away. "I like having lots of stuff around me." With that, Charlie led us into the next room to see his prized set of antique dueling pistols.

From then on, I made a point of visiting Charlie's house whenever a chance presented itself, and I never failed to come away with a good story or ten. Conversations with Charlie moved easily through decades and generations, woven together with threads of daring, ingenuity, and surprise. All memory is selective and every autobiography is abridged. What we leave out can be as revealing as what we put in. Charlie's narrative was relentlessly upbeat. His nostalgia somehow opened new possibilities; his past was a forward-looking place.

I noticed, for instance, that World War I and the influenza pandemic of 1918 never surfaced in his stories, though both of these terrible events came close to him. It must have been a stirring sight for a boy of twelve or thirteen to watch young men just a few years older march off to save Europe from its self-made catastrophe. One of them, a boy six years older than Charlie with a job at the *Kansas City Star,* was Ernest Hemingway.

The troops were led by a local hero. Close enough, anyway. Kansas City laid claim to the handsome General John J. Pershing—"Black Jack"—commander of the American Expeditionary Force. Born one hundred miles away in Laclede, Missouri, the dashing general had recently filled newspapers with his exploits in pursuit of Mexican revolutionary Pancho Villa. Pershing's subsequent success in Europe earned him the exalted rank of General of the Armies of the United States, the first since George Washington. There has yet to be another (though legislation proposed in 2021 would award the rank posthumously to Ulysses S. Grant). After the Great War, Kansas City honored Pershing with a grand memorial to the fallen, raising $2.5 million in ten days from local residents to fund the construction. A mighty tower, with a glowing flame on top, rose on the hill where young Charlie White had watched Union Station take shape a few years earlier.

The flu pandemic was a local story, too. The ferocious bug was ultimately traced to a training camp for U.S. troops in rural Kansas. Shipped to the battlefield via Union Station, young men in army twill carried the virus across the country and to Europe, shedding germs as they went. One-third of the world's population was eventually infected; cities were shut down; morgues swamped with corpses. Citizens protested orders to stay home and to wear masks in public. Nearly 700,000 Americans died, many in the prime of life.

These were among the most dramatic events of the twentieth century. But they weren't Charlie's story. While all that death and suffering was darkening the world, Charlie was in the sunrise of his life. He seemed to have appreciated, even in high school, that he would only be young once, and he would not waste this experience on the funeral pyres of war and disease. Instead, at sixteen, in his senior year, he dreamed up his own declaration of independence.

An odyssey to California in the dawn of automobiles became Charlie's defining story. On my trips to see him, I heard this tale more often than any other. He cherished it and returned to it like a talisman, as though a century could be evoked through the memory of one seminal experience.

From his days leaping campfires in fringed leather leggings, Charlie had been infected with the same fever that created Kansas City: to go west. The human waves that rolled over the tribal lands of the Native Americans—the wagon trains and the pushcart pioneers—gathered and launched from Kansas City. They rode west if they could afford it, walked west if they could not, through oceans of grass as high as their shoulders, across deserts as dry as their jerky, over mountains as steep as their dreams. Always west, chasing the sunset.

Their ghosts were still young when Charlie arrived in Kansas City, the place where East ended and West began, where Lewis and Clark pushed into the Louisiana Purchase, front door to the greatest land steal and real estate deal in the history of the world. First came the trailblazing Boone family, Daniel and his sons; then the mountain man Jim Bridger, the scout Kit Carson, the prophet Brigham Young, the doomed Donner Party: all the seekers of gold and silver and freedom and topsoil; the bison killers, the Bible thumpers—countless thousands of future-chasing Americans traveling by riverboat and wagon and railroad, Westward Ho!, through the place where the Kaw River poured itself into the Missouri at the vital center of a continent. The place where the great western trails—the California Trail, the Santa Fe Trail, the Oregon Trail—all began.

This past met the future in Charlie's odyssey. You see, not long after Charlie's eighth birthday, the Ford Motor Company introduced one of the most transformative innovations in economic history: the industrial assembly line. Ford's new factory in Highland Park, Michigan, cut the time needed to build an automobile body by 75 percent. Additional lines were rapidly added to work similar wonders in the production of engines, transmissions, and wheel assemblies.

A Model T Ford that required twelve hours to build in 1912 rolled off the line in a mere ninety-three minutes by 1916. This enormous gain in efficiency allowed Ford to nearly double the wages of its workers while cutting the price of each car by one-third.

The Model T knocked America for a loop. Cheap, sturdy, and easy to repair, these simple cars—available in every color, it was said, provided the color was black—unleashed something primal in the human genome. For thousands of years, humans had moved at walking speeds over walking distances. Now this huffing, sputtering machine remade geography, economies, societies. Highways, service stations, truck plazas, motels, fast-food restaurants, shopping malls, suburbs: all were the product of this one invention, the affordable, dependable automobile. It was pure freedom, to go as one wished and stop as one would.

Before the Highland Park assembly line, one in every one hundred Americans owned a car. Nine years later, in 1921, that number had grown by more than 800 percent, to nearly one in ten. Roughly half of all cars owned by Americans were Model Ts, many of them assembled in Ford's second modern plant, opened in Kansas City in 1913.

The Model T was, in every meaningful sense, the birth of the automobile age and the cradle of car culture; therefore, it was another seismic shift in Charlie's world. Cars would change the way people shopped, the way they ate, the way they courted, the way they died. Cars would change where they lived and how they socialized and whether they knew their neighbors. Cars would alter the physical fitness of human bodies, and change the smell of the air they breathed. The ripe stench of horse manure gave way to the acrid hint of exhaust, and the rattle of wagon wheels was replaced by the hum and cough of combustion engines.

This volcano of change was just breaking through the cultural mantle when Charlie was in high school. He was entranced, caught in freedom's spell. Charlie and two buddies from school hatched a secret scheme to drive a Model T from Kansas City to Los Angeles.

For adults, this was an audacious idea—much less for a trio of boys. Where roads existed at all, they were atrocious: unpaved, rutted, muddy, or dusty. Many rivers were unbridged. Forget about creeks. Traffic laws were nonexistent.

Floyd Field was one of the earliest automotive argonauts. A dean at Georgia Tech, he set out from Atlanta for Oregon one summer just after World War I. Creeping cross-country in a Model T that his students dubbed "the Rambling Wreck," Field needed five weeks in each direction. Nature set the speed limit: roughly seventy miles per day along unmarked roads, across trackless lava beds, groaning over mountain passes, and jolting down wagon ruts worn in endless prairies. Thanks to the dean's cheerful endurance and the car's robust components, the Ramblin' Wreck of Georgia Tech is celebrated to this day.

The boys had a similar trip in mind. They knew—or thought they knew—how rough the journey could be. Kansas City's roads were notoriously bad. The same year Charlie and his friends finished high school, a young artist a few years older named Walt Disney was trying to get a business started not far from Charlie's house. Working in a new art form known as "animation," Disney sold a series of short films to the Newman Theater downtown, cartoon commentaries on local issues that Disney called "Laugh-o-Grams." The vignettes played before main feature films on nights when the Newman's vaudeville stage was silent. One Disney animation poked fun at the dangers of driving in Kansas City. The young artist sketched two passengers in "a flivver"——a Model T—flying several feet above their car as one wheel caromed off an outcropping while another sank into a pothole.

Audiences were charmed by the novel shorts, which almost seemed alive. But Disney's Kansas City business failed to take wing, and so like Charlie, young Disney struck out for California—though Disney chose to go by train.

An organization based in Kansas City was determined to make America a nation of automobiles. The National Old Trails Road Association——the name evoked the original wagon trains—enlisted car enthusiasts to lobby for the first continuous paved road stretching from coast to coast. The proposed route would follow the path of the original National Road from Maryland into Illinois. From there the road would pick up the trail blazed by the Boone family across Missouri. At Kansas City, the route would adopt the tried-and-true course of the Santa Fe Trail through Kansas, across the Rockies, southward into New Mexico, and over the desert southwest to Los Angeles. To publicize the route, the Old Trails Association placed markers on fence posts, trees, and boulders along the dirt byways and narrow farm roads leading west to the Pacific. The association also published a guidebook to the trail, noting which drugstores along the way sold gasoline and which general stores sold replacement tires. There were tips for finding the route: bear left at the whitewashed farmhouse, or jog right at the twisted stump. That sort of thing.

One of Charlie's high school fraternity brothers was a boy named Bob Long, whose father was, Charlie told me, "a well-to-do real estate man." Long owned a 1917 Model T touring car with bicycle fenders, Chesterfield seats, and a fold-up canopy. Itching to take his car cross-country, Long invited Charlie and another fraternity brother, Edgar Snow, to set out for California after their high school graduation in May 1922.

Long had chosen his partners well. As plucky as Charlie was, Edgar Snow was that much more so. He and Charlie had bonded as the youngest members of their high school class and, always eager to prove themselves, they shared a sense of the world's possibilities. Snow aspired to a career of travel and discovery, going where others wouldn't dare and writing the stories he found—the bigger the stories, the better. When Snow wasn't typing away on his fraternity newspaper, he was nurturing the dreams of an incorrigible explorer. Bob Long's proposed trip to California took the place of Snow's long-held notion of rafting down the Mississippi.

Snow couldn't know then—but might have hoped—that this Tin Lizzie exploit would be the beginning of a career that eventually made him one of the world's most famous foreign correspondents. His "scoop of the century," as it was widely known, would come not much more than a decade later, when the young journalist tracked down an insurgent leader in the remote Chinese interior. Snow's experience as the first Westerner to interview Mao Zedong was told in his blockbuster bestselling book, *Red Star Over China,* published in 1937. Later accused of communist sympathies during the Red-baiting 1950s, Snow took up a self-imposed exile in Switzerland, where his boyhood chum Charlie White paid him a visit. Snow's final exclusive, published in 1970 on the cover of *Time,* was another interview with Mao, long after his victory in the civil war. The aging dictator used Snow's return to extend an invitation to President Richard M. Nixon to visit China. The rest is history.

But that's nearly fifty years compressed into a few sentences.

Returning to 1922, we find three boys, one journey, and two stumbling blocks.

The first impediment was their parents. According to Charlie, Long was reluctant to ask his folks to allow the journey. He suspected they would say no. Subscribing to the philosophy that it's easier to beg forgiveness than to ask permission, Long needed a ruse to cover his departure. Charlie, on the other hand, was sure that his mother would cheerfully approve the trip if he asked her, but he took subversive joy in helping Long stage a deception.

Stumbling block number two led them to their ruse. Charlie and Ed Snow had no money to spare for the trip. But the winter wheat was ready for harvest on the Kansas prairie. Demand for field hands was high. The boys told their parents they were going to make some money for college. Their unspoken plan was to keep going west once their pockets were filled.

⌒

They set out in late spring of 1922, two boys on the front bench of the car, the third sprawled across the bench in back. Moving not much faster than a jog, they jostled slowly out of town in the wake of the wagon trains, across lightly marked fields, over the grass-blown Flint Hills, and onto the high, flat plains. They picked their way from marker to marker with only the Old Trails guidebook to help them. "There were really no roads, no maps," Charlie recalled. "We had a sort of a directory which would say, 'Go ten miles this way, and you'll find a big hemlock tree and turn right'—that sort of direction."

At nearly every crossroads, they saw hand-painted signs advertising farm work at six dollars per day. Wealthy Bob Long had plenty of cash, as Charlie remembered it, and kept driving until they reached a town large enough to boast a handsome hotel, where he rented a room and passed the time while Charlie and Ed got busy on a farm nearby. "From sunup to sundown, we worked in that hot sun stacking wheat," Charlie recalled.

The city boys had a lot to learn. On their first day, the youngest graduates of Westport High were introduced to a primitive device called a header. An open drum of whirling blades pulled by four horses harnessed abreast, the machine cut wheat and sent it up a rattling conveyor belt to fall into a horse-drawn wagon moving slowly alongside. Leading the horses through the scratchy fields was hard work. Wheat dust filled the boys' noses and powdered their sweat-wet bodies. When the big wagon could hold no more, the boys drove it to a central gathering place where they bundled and stacked the crop in sheaves for the thresher.

"We slept on the ground," Charlie told me. "We were so exhausted. Sometimes we got a bath in a horse tank." Though I heard Charlie tell this story a number of times, I never dulled to his marvelous self-confidence. Not only had he set out at age sixteen to cross the country on unpaved roads. Not only had he done it without letting anyone know where he was going or when he would return. He did it with empty pockets, sure that he could make his way somehow. Though he knew next to nothing about farming, he had faith in his own ability to learn quickly and to work hard. "It was funny," Charlie mused, "because we were just high school kids. We didn't understand how to harness horses and all. When we first went out there, the farmers threw us a set of harnesses at four o'clock in the morning and said: 'Harness the horses.' We had a terrible time! We got that harness on backwards." He chuckled at the memory.

"We finally manipulated it, and became expert in a few days—like high school kids will."

I loved that line: *Like high school kids will.* Charlie and his intrepid friend Ed not only had the courage they needed; they also understood the strengths they brought to the table. Older workers could beat them on skill and experience, but they made up for it with their eagerness to grow and adapt. Resourcefulness is a close cousin of resilience. Rather than be defeated in advance by their lack of experience and credentials, the boys were resourceful about leveraging the material at hand—starting with the learning attitude of youth.

After a week and a half in the wheat fields, Charlie and Ed were pretty solid farmhands, with hardened muscles and fifty bucks apiece. They could feel the money burning in their pockets. "We said, 'We're wealthy!'" Charlie recalled. "'Let's go to California!'"

Driving a Model T Ford was quite unlike the experience of driving today. To start the car, the driver or a passenger inserted a detachable hand crank into the engine through a slot below the front grille, and after adjusting the choke and priming the carburetor, gave a vigorous half turn. Ideally this caused a small magneto to generate sufficient electrical current to ignite the fuel in the first cylinder and bring the engine to life. Cranking was among the most dangerous aspects of early motoring, because if the mix of fuel and air was wrong the engine could backfire, jerking the crank violently and causing a broken wrist. Once it was chugging properly, the Ford's four-cylinder in-line engine—which came to be called a "four-banger"—generated 20 horsepower, impressive for the time; this energy was translated to the rear wheels through a two-speed transmission.

Inside the car, the driver confronted two small levers projecting from the steering column. These weren't turn indicators or wiper controls, because neither blinkers nor windshield wipers were standard features on the Model T. Instead the left-hand lever controlled the engine's timing while the right-hand lever regulated speed.

From the floor of the vehicle rose three metal pedals and one large lever. Operated together, these put the car in gear. By depressing the leftmost pedal and shifting the lever, the driver moved from neutral into low gear and then into high. The middle pedal was for backing up. The pedal on the right controlled the brake, which worked by friction on the transmission drum. (There was no gas pedal—remember, the accelerator was mounted on the steering column.)

Assuming the driver mastered the elaborate dance of pedal pressing and lever pushing, the Model T could reach speeds of 40 and even 45 miles per hour, given a patch of smooth road and a favorable wind. The route to Los Angeles covered about 1,700 miles—or about 42 hours of driving at 40 mph. However, the Tin Lizzie rarely hit top speed. On the rough, unpaved pathways of the western United States, travelers were delighted to make half that rate, while slowing even further for obstructions, dead ends, and wrong turns. Breakdowns were always a danger. Engines overheated. A severe rut could crack one of the Ford's wooden artillery wheels. Passing horses—the primary occupants of these roads—left horseshoe nails scattered in their paths, menacing the thin-walled rubber tires of the Model T.

But the boys weren't in any hurry. They dubbed themselves "the Unconscious Three" and liked the sobriquet so much that they painted the words on the side of Long's car. Feeling every bump and jostle through the stiff steel of the suspension, and rocking on the bouncy bedsprings beneath the bench upholstery, they puttered off to explore the wide world.

⌒⌒

There were two proven paths across Kansas for an automobile in 1922. Unfortunately, I didn't learn this fact until after Charlie was gone. I would have liked to double-check which route they followed. He talked about their guidebook, so I took for granted that they chose the Old Trails route. A. L. Westgard, author of America's first books on transcontinental automobile travel, wrote of this path, "it takes first place, looked at either from the standpoint of surface condition, scenery, historic interest or hotel accommodations."

The route would have had particular appeal to Charlie and Ed Snow. It took them through Emporia, Kansas, where the aspiring journalist Snow could have picked up a copy of the world-renowned local newspaper, the *Emporia Gazette*. Its editor, William Allen White, was certainly the most famous man in Kansas at the time, perhaps the most famous in the entire Midwest. For half a century, White's editorials were reprinted and read from coast to coast, and such personages as former president Theodore Roosevelt and the movie star Douglas Fairbanks had been known to visit his stately Emporia home, called Red Rocks.

White was very much in the news as the boys passed through Kansas, for he was embroiled in a crusade against the newly popular Ku Klux Klan, which was spreading its populist poison across the American heartland. In the aftermath of the war in Europe and the sharp recession of 1920, a resurgent Klan promised to defend "100 percent Americanism" against immigrants and nonwhite citizens.

White used the pages of his newspaper to denounce the vulgar appeal of the Klan, and when that soapbox seemed too limited, the Emporia editor ran for governor of Kansas in 1924 on an anti-Klan platform. His eventual loss was an embarrassment to Kansas, and the backlash may have helped to break the fever of hatred. But in 1922, the divisions were wide and hot.

For Charlie, with his appetite for tales of the Old West, a way station farther along the road would have held more appeal. Dodge City, Kansas, was the last and most legendary of the nineteenth-century cattle drive boomtowns, where gunslingers Wyatt Earp and Bat Masterson frequented the Long Branch Saloon while aiming to avoid a long stay at Boot Hill Cemetery. During a brief but colorful few decades after the Civil War, Texas cattle ranchers shipped their beef to urban markets by driving the steers up the Chisholm Trail to connect with the new railroad across Kansas. But during those same years, homesteading farmers were filling the Kansas prairie, pushing the cattle drives farther and farther to the west. Abilene, the original destination for Texas beef, gave way to Ellsworth, which became known as "the wickedest" town on the open range during its brief and bloody heyday. Then the cowboys were shunted again, to Dodge City, dubbed the "Sodom of the West."

It was there, in the election of 1883, that townsfolk installed a crowd of reformers to clean up the drinking and the fighting and the whoring that made the town infamous—starting with the Long Branch Saloon. Authorities raided the barroom and brothel and put it out of business. Get out of Dodge, the reformers told Luke Short, proprietor and pimp, but Short merely decamped to Kansas City long enough to recruit some friends who were handy with pistols. By the time Short returned with Masterson, Earp, and a few others, the Dodge City economy was slumping under the weight of a lot of unhappy cowboys. The town prigs were reconsidering their rash flirtation with virtue. After a brief negotiation, Short reopened the Long Branch without firing a shot. He and his gunslingers commemorated their victory by posing for what became a famous photograph, widely known for its ironic caption: the Dodge City Peace Commission.

Such stories conjure the jangling spurs and barroom pianos of Hollywood cliché. For the boys in the Model T, however, those days weren't even forty years in the past. In fact, if the boys motored down the dusty main street where the famed gunfighters had once steered horses, they did so at a time when Bat Masterson and Wyatt Earp were still alive. Masterson was a sports columnist for a New York City newspaper in 1922, author of the memorable observation that "we all get the same amount of ice. The rich get it in the summertime, and the poor get it in the winter." The less quotable, equally colorful Earp worked as a consultant on sets of silent movie westerns, midwifing his own legend.

West of Dodge, the boys would have chugged along the cusp between past and future, across land where seemingly infinite herds of bison had roamed just a few decades earlier. They would have puttered through towns where old men could recall Comanche raiding parties and cavalry reprisals. The land was immense, and the sky even larger, stretching from one flat horizon to the other. Puffing trains of the Atchison, Topeka & Santa Fe Railway appeared behind them as mere smudges on the eastern horizon, overtook them gradually, then pulled past in clouds of smoke and cinders. The sun tracked the same course, baking the boys on the black leather seats.

Among Charlie's papers after he died was the transcript of an interview that Bob Long gave to Edgar Snow's biographer nearly sixty years after the trip. The way Long remembered it, the Unconscious Three crossed Kansas on a more northerly route near what became Interstate 70. Long said they followed the less famous Midland Trail, carved by the miners of the 1859 Colorado gold rush, as far as Colorado Springs at the foot of Pikes Peak. Then, by Long's account, they turned south rather than cross the forbidding Central Rockies and soon joined the Old Trails route near La Junta, Colorado, not far from the place on Sand Creek where settlers from the same generation as the boys' grandparents massacred Cheyenne and Arapahoe women and children as they camped peacefully in 1864.

The adventurers stopped for food and fuel at tiny general stores. "There were no gas stations," Charlie told me. "You got your gas at a grocery store. There were no rest stops, either. As I remember, there were no places to sleep. We just slept on the ground. Of course, if it was raining, we got underneath the car."

When they drove past sundown, their headlamps, powered by the little magneto, brightened and dimmed according to their speed. "If you were going to drive at night, you had to drive at least twenty-five miles an hour to get enough power," Charlie explained. "The faster you drove, the better your lights were. But the roads were so bad, it would bounce you out of the car almost."

Now their route passed through the coalfields of southern Colorado, notorious for the violence and oppression of the labor uprisings there. Eight years earlier, Colorado's governor had dispatched the National Guard to break up a tent city of striking miners known as the Ludlow encampment. Employees of the Colorado Fuel &

Iron Company, the strikers—mostly immigrants and African-Americans—were defying an owner whose very name was synonymous with wealth and power: John D. Rockefeller Jr. The guardsmen arrived on horseback and in an armored car with mounted machine gun. They took position on a ridge over the camp and opened fire. At least seven miners were killed. More than a dozen women and children took cover in a bunker, where they suffocated when the guardsmen torched the tents above them. The Ludlow Massacre, as the tragedy came to be known, sparked retaliatory killings of mine guards, foremen, and managers throughout the region in a war that raged until President Woodrow Wilson sent regular U.S. Army troops to restore order.

Charlie recalled only the gradual change of scenery as they motored through La Junta, an early trading station on the Santa Fe Trail. After hundreds of miles of gray-brown prairie, they entered the green shrubland of the high chaparral. In the western distance, the jagged Sangre de Cristo Mountains filled the horizon like a purple wave foamed with snow. If the boys had been climbers, they would have found on that horizon some of the most forbidding peaks of the entire Rocky Mountain chain. Instead they turned their chugging buggy south, keeping the mountains on their right, puttering toward an easier crossing.

A week into the trip, the boys blew out a tire. With no jack in the car, Ed Snow, the strongest of the three, strained to lift one corner of the vehicle high enough to let the other boys slip on the spare. Wary of another blowout, they crept along to the next town, where they bought four replacements at the general store.

They couldn't parallel the mountains forever. Their crossing point came as they neared the New Mexico border and the road began climbing toward Raton Pass. As the grade steepened, the four-banger strained and whined. "I remember it was so steep that the car wouldn't make it. So one guy drove while the other two would get out and push on the car," Charlie said. Taking turns behind the wheel, "we literally pushed the car over Raton Pass. But the car was so light, and we were pretty strong kids."

Their sweat dried quickly in the cool mountain air as they raced down the south side of the pass. "Should the tourist be fortunate enough to see a sunset while descending the mountain, he will always remember its magnificence," wrote A. L. Westgard—though he added a warning that drivers would soon be dodging "natural obstacles in the way of adobe soil, lava rocks and sandy stretches" that would be "greater tasks to overcome than are to be found in most states."

At the little village of Las Vegas, New Mexico—which was nevertheless nearly twice the size of the flyspeck town in Nevada that shared its name—their route turned westerly again, across the remote scrubland and deserts of the Southwest. This was the newest, rawest, most alien land in the continental United States. In the space of two months in 1912—just ten years earlier—New Mexico and Arizona had added their stars to the flag, numbers 47 and 48. Together the two states were three and a half times the size of Missouri, but home to barely one-fifth as many people. Sparse Kansas had seven times the population density of these wild and open places, where Spanish and Navajo were about as widely spoken as English.

The mesas and pinnacles of this countryside were strange to the wide-eyed travelers, as were the adobe plazas of the Spanish missions and the domed hogans of the Navajo shepherds. Raised on jingoistic stories of Indian savages, the boys were now among the Native Americans, motoring slowly over the land of the Zuni, the Navajo, and the Hopi. They found the original inhabitants to be welcoming hosts. "We ended up in Indian camps in the evening, and they'd give us snake meat and things like that," Charlie told me. I wondered if he might be embellishing the tale until I learned that a traditional Zuni delicacy in late springtime is fried locusts with sweet corn bread.

West of the mountains, the rough roads grew rougher—"not even gravel, just dirt and sand," Charlie remembered. When the Ford got stuck, as it did more than once, the car was light enough for the boys to tug and shove it loose. Drivers of larger vehicles weren't so lucky; the Unconscious Three passed hulks of heavy automobiles rooted in the soft ground. "We saw car after car—with the big cars, they'd get stuck, and they couldn't get out."

On a desolate stretch in sun-beaten Arizona, their car broke down. Charlie recalled ninety years later that a wheel bearing "burned out." The memory of being stranded in that harsh place was as vivid as yesterday. "We were fifty miles from nowhere, and practically no traffic," Charlie said. "We were just sitting around. We didn't know what to do. We sat there for about an hour."

Maybe it was three hours.

Maybe it was five.

After whatever period of time, "along came a farmer in a little Model T Ford, a little pickup," Charlie recalled. One of the remarkable qualities of the Model T—a reason for its incredible success— was that this one mechanical platform could easily be adapted to multiple uses. The touring car of wealthy Bob Long could be transformed in short order into the original Ford truck driven by this Arizona farmer, simply by unbolting the backseat with its bedsprings and installing in its place a sturdy wooden box. What's more, the workings of a Model T were simple enough to be understood by any reasonably confident tinkerer.

A century later, automobiles are infinitely more complex, and a person needs specialized expertise and equipment to go much beyond changing the oil or refilling the wiper fluid. But it remains important, I think, for people to have some basic knowledge of the technology in our lives, just as Charlie and his friends had an understanding of their broken car. Students should be encouraged to learn how to build a simple website, just as they might learn to replace a leaky faucet, and plant a garden. Competence breeds confidence; it is an antidote to the feeling that change is a hostile force sweeping the world along helpless in its current.

"What's the matter, boys?" called the farmer as he slowed his truck.

"We burned a wheel out, the bearings on a wheel," Charlie remembered their reply.

To their surprise and relief, the farmer said: "That happened to me last month." He pulled to the roadside and, reaching into his wooden truck box, produced the needed part, saying, "I've got a spare right here."

"So he gave us the spare bearing, and we put that in and went on," Charlie recalled. "And you say the Lord wasn't with us?"

Perhaps more dangerous in the unforgiving desert, the car overheated one day, "scoring"—that is, scratching—an engine cylinder. Only as the radiator boiled dry did the boys realize they had run out of water. Miles from the nearest town, they had to get the car running again or risk heatstroke, even death. They let the engine cool, then poured their last bottle of soda pop into the radiator. The way it foamed did not inspire confidence, but the plan worked well enough for them to creep to the next general store.

Farther along, after an overnight stop in the Mojave Desert, the boys awoke to find a Native American man sitting silently beside their car, wearing a blanket over his shoulders in the early morning chill. He was waiting patiently to say hello. They shared their breakfast with him, and complimented his English. He surprised them further by replying that he had a degree from Harvard.

After two weeks on the road, averaging perhaps ten miles per hour, the Unconscious Three rolled in their dusty Ford down the western slope of the San Gabriel Mountains and into the town of Los Angeles. Compared with what it was to become, this great city of the twentieth century was, Charlie remembered, "just a small town. Los Angeles was a few houses and in between were orange trees. Oranges all around, orange groves."

The trio had crossed half a continent in a contraption not much more complex than a lawn mower to gaze for the first time at the sea. They sought no permission and needed no help beyond their own gumption and the kindness of a few strangers. But now, with that deflation so familiar to travelers, they realized that getting there had consumed all their foresight and energy. Once they stopped, they faced the question of how to get home.

Among the three of them, they knew one person in all of California— and only barely. Charles "Buddy" Rogers was a year older than Charlie White and hailed from Olathe, Kansas, a day's round-trip from Kansas

City by horse-and-buggy. When both boys were children, a streetcar line forged a link between the big city and nearby Kansas communities, which opened a world of possibilities for Olathe farmboys. Buddy Rogers seized the possibilities of the Kansas City music scene to hone his talents as a performer, and the Westport boys had probably met him at a concert or dance. They absorbed the news with interest when Rogers left school to move with his mother to Hollywood and take a shot at the movie business.

Quite a shot it turned out to be. Within five years of leaving Olathe, Buddy Rogers was a huge star, famous as "America's Boy Friend." In 1927 he made Hollywood history as the leading man opposite Clara Bow in *Wings*—the first winner of the Academy Award for Best Picture. Later, his affair with actress Mary Pickford would contribute to her sensational divorce from the swashbuckling superstar Douglas Fairbanks in 1936. Rogers's subsequent marriage to Pickford was, by contrast, among the most durable in show business, lasting until Pickford's death in 1979. In 1982, the Academy of Motion Picture Arts and Sciences again honored Buddy Rogers with an award for humanitarian work—an award also given, over the years, to such stars as Paul Newman, Frank Sinatra, Audrey Hepburn, and Angelina Jolie.

That all lay in the future. For now, Buddy Rogers was an unknown teenager with a dream. And here were three boys from Kansas City, passing acquaintances, on his doorstep. Somehow the travelers tracked him to "a little cottage there in Los Angeles," Charlie recalled, where Rogers was living while learning the film trade. When Charlie explained how they got there, Rogers invited the trio in and fed them breakfast. The travelers lingered long enough to bivouac for the night, but the next morning "we decided we weren't going to live off of Buddy," Charlie recalled. Rogers and his mother no doubt encouraged that decision.

For a day or two, Charlie said, they cadged free food by attending real estate pitches, pretending to be on a scouting trip for their parents interested in California investments. And bakeries offered free samples—at least until the bakers caught on to these repeat visitors. Neither ploy was a lasting solution, and soon the need to get home grew pressing.

For Long, the return trip was simply a matter of throwing himself on the mercy of his parents. He sold the battered Ford for a few bucks, checked into a hotel, and wired his folks for help. His exasperated mother rushed by train to Los Angeles to fetch him.

Charlie and Ed were on their own. Their wheat-reaping money was exhausted. Their rich friend's Model T was gone. Buddy Rogers's door was closed, and they had run through the supply of soft-hearted real estate agents. "We thought, well, we'll just hop trains," Charlie explained.

Only one imperfection marred this plan: "We'd never hopped a train before."

After hoofing it to the Los Angeles freight yards, the boys crept silently across the sidings in search of an eastbound train. They knew enough about railroads to understand that they should catch the train as it was moving, to diminish the chance of being caught. But the train should not be moving very quickly, because speed multiplied the substantial danger of climbing onto a mountain of metal in motion. The ideal train for hopping would be one just getting under way.

Spotting a likely target, they crouched until it lurched to life with a screech of wheels. They burst from hiding, sprinted along the tracks, and swung themselves onto a car. Exhilarated and proud, they settled back for the ride—only to find they were traveling in the wrong direction. "We hopped on a freight train we thought was going east, but it was going north," Charlie said years later with a chuckle.

After a full day on the rails, the train stopped "up near San Francisco." It was a good news–bad news day for Charlie and Ed. The two friends had learned to catch a train—the good news—but they were no closer to home. And their poverty was acute.

As they walked from the railyard in search of a meager meal, the boys discovered they had taken up life on the rails in the middle of one of the worst labor strikes ever to hit American railroads. Having nationalized the train industry during wartime, the federal government was now returning the rails to private control. Operators were determined to cut costs. A proposed 12 percent reduction in pay for shop workers provoked a coast-to-coast walkout.

The boys learned of this from signs around the railyard. The rail companies had set up camps for replacement workers—so-called scabs—to keep the trains rolling in spite of the strike. One sign advertised for waiters and busboys to work at one of the scab camps. "The sign said they needed help in waiting tables for the Mexican workers that were refrigerating the cars to carry produce to the East," Charlie remembered. Following directions on the sign, the penniless travelers arrived at a gate in a high-security fence somewhere in Oakland. Armed guards, working for the Western Pacific Railroad, eyed the boys up and down, then waved them by. They presented themselves to the hiring authorities.

For the next ten days, Charlie and Ed served food to replacement workers inside modified passenger railcars. The pay was three dollars per day plus meals and a place to sleep. Each day their pockets grew a bit heavier, and when they each had thirty dollars, they calculated that it was enough to see them safely home.

Now they were in enough of a hurry to risk hopping a passenger train. Back in the yard, they found one building its head of steam. After waiting for the whistle that signaled closing doors, they darted to the rear of a car and grabbed the ladder that led to the roof. Clambering to the top of the compartment as it lurched to life, they flattened themselves to avoid being seen from the ground. The rolling, jerking mass beneath them gradually gained speed.

The train headed eastward from the Bay Area, away from the setting sun, then turned north through Sacramento and Oroville before orienting again to the east. Night cloaked the stowaways as the train climbed the Sierra Nevada through Feather River Canyon. Neither boy was prepared for the sharp drop in temperature as night fell over the mountains. They shivered and huddled together. "Ed and I strapped ourselves to the top of this passenger car, and we about froze to death going through the canyon at night," Charlie ruefully recalled.

They weren't cold for long. Dawn found the miserable boys descending from the mountains into the Black Rock Desert of northern Nevada, where the mercury climbs past 90 on an average July day. After the long night spent rolling between walls of pine trees and past cliffs of bare rock, the openness of the desert was weird and shocking. Black Rock is a stupendous table covered in dun-colored chalk dust, a seeming stage prepared for titanic performers to enact a drama for an audience of distant, haze-shrouded peaks. I never told

Charlie what became of that emptiness, but by the time I knew him, the desert was famous as the scene of the annual "Burning Man" festival, a bacchanalia of art and mysticism, drugs and sex, futurism and atavism, that draws some sixty-five thousand people each summer. I don't know that he would have believed me.

For when his train stopped, there was nothing but a lonely water tower where the engine's thirsty boilers drank their fill. The boys were alarmed to see the brakeman hop into the dust and start down the train, inspecting each car. As he reached theirs, he spotted the boys on the roof and ordered them to the ground. They protested against being left in the desert, but the railroad man wasn't listening. The train's water tanks were almost full; the whistle blew a warning as the brakeman continued his walk toward the caboose.

A quick look around the sunbaked expanse convinced the stowaways that they had no choice. "We couldn't be stranded out there in the desert," Charlie reasoned. After a whispered conference, Charlie and Ed sauntered away as if they were heading for a tiny settlement in the distance. When they managed to put the train between themselves and the brakeman, they crept "like Indians" to the engine and watched the movements of their nemesis through the gap between track and carriage.

Above them, the boilers were now full and the blaze inside the firebox was raising a fresh head of steam. Protruding from the front of the engine, like whiskers on a chin, was a metal prow known as the cowcatcher. The name told its purpose: if a train on some remote prairie encountered a herd of animals across the tracks, this device might urge the beasts to scatter as the engine crept forward. Its wedge also worked to shove downed trees, small boulders, and even snow from the tracks. Best of all, from the boys' perspective, the angles of the engine prevented the men in the cab from seeing the cowcatcher below.

Shooting another glance under the cars, the boys saw the brakeman's feet disappear as he climbed back onto the train. Charlie and Ed darted forward to the cowcatcher and climbed aboard. "I guess we rode the next hundred and fifty miles that way," Charlie recounted.

This cat-and-mouse game continued across half a continent. "We'd get kicked off, and bounced off. And then we'd get another train," Charlie said. The strike made everything more difficult, because extra guards had been hired to prevent sabotage. Charlie and Ed learned every niche and hideaway on the outside of a train. The steps of a passenger car made a kingly throne—but also the first place guards would look as a train pulled into a station. The cowcatcher was a thrill, with the massive force of a roaring train pushing it forward. But it was terribly uncomfortable after three or four hours— and extremely dangerous. "The ordinary place to hide," Charlie told me, "was the little vacant area behind the coal car, between the coal car and the express car. That was an area where they weren't looking much. That's where we'd hide."

Even this lair had its drawbacks. Each time the train passed through a tunnel—and there were dozens of tunnels as the trains rose into the Rockies—"these coal-burning trains blew hot ashes" from their funnels into the tunnel ceilings and back down onto the train. "I can still remember those hot ashes coming down on us," Charlie told me.

Once or twice, the hired guards found them. "We called them 'train dicks,'" said Charlie of the men who hauled him and his friend from the station to the jail. "They'd keep us there all night, give us a good breakfast, and then kick us out."

At several points along the way, Charlie and Ed found themselves in camps with men who lived on the rails. The boys didn't like the way they were eyed up and down. "I had a wristwatch," Charlie recalled. "The first time we stopped at a hobo camp, one of the guys said, 'Sonny, you'd better take that off. Somebody will kill you for it.'

"After that, I carried my wristwatch on my ankle."

Charlie recounted this entire California odyssey several times during my visits across the street. After a couple of tellings, I realized that he never mentioned fear. I began to picture the menace of the train yards; the heedless tonnage of the moving cars with their amputating wheels. I imagined the deadly desert heat; the cramping fingers clutching the cowcatcher. I pictured men who would cut a boy's throat for a wristwatch. Why wasn't Charlie afraid?

I came to believe that, of course, he was scared. But how else was he going to get home? There's a wonderful exchange in George R. R. Martin's epic *Game of Thrones*. Bran asks his father, "Can a man still be brave if he's afraid?" His father replies, "That is the only time a man can be brave." And Charlie understood that telling stories of bravery makes bravery easier. Our stories can be told in major or minor keys. We can dwell on defeat or on determination. We can stress setbacks or successes. Charlie insisted on the joyful version of his life, and I believe it made him a happier person.

Always the story ended with the same parting image. The boys were riding a flatcar belonging to the Missouri Pacific Railroad, the line that would finally take them home. And they were the only passengers. "I remember coming through the Colorado Rockies," said

Charlie. "And I remember Ed and I lying there as we went through the Royal Gorge."

A ten-mile canyon of breathtaking cliffs and chasms carved over trackless time by the Arkansas River, the gorge narrows the sky to an azure ribbon and wraps the river in walls of rock. The boys must have known that beyond that scene their journey would have its drab denouement amid scrub and prairie leading to a place that would never be quite the same: home. For that glorious moment they were brother knights of a splendid kingdom. "Well, now! What could be more luxurious?" said Charlie to Ed, or Ed to Charlie. "We have a car all to ourselves." On their backs they took in the narrow sky as the train made gentle curves along the riverbank. Cotton ball clouds floated from one canyon rim to the other. Across nearly a century, Charlie could see it all in his mind's eye undimmed. "And I remember saying, 'Boy, this is the life.'"

six

The year I met Charlie was also the year Apple introduced the first iPhone. I didn't immediately understand the fuss. Perhaps because I write for a living, and started so long ago that I used a typewriter, I've always related to computers initially as fancy typing devices. The iPhone's tiny touchscreen keyboard struck me as a lousy way to type.

This was an epic example of missing the point, I admit. If I had been around when humans harnessed fire, I might have complained that the early adopters were burning up perfectly good wooden clubs. Charlie wouldn't make that mistake. He understood that thriving through change begins with an eagerness for The New.

When Charlie and his friend Ed Snow rode that Missouri Pacific Railroad flatcar out of the Royal Gorge and onto the high prairie, they were heading home to something very new. Like the smartphone, the revolutionary technology of 1922 was a device that erased distance, sparked creativity, upended culture, and empowered celebrity. It came to be known as "radio," but in its early days the miracle of wireless communication was so novel that even its name was up for grabs. A few months earlier, on February 16, 1922, the *Kansas City Star* announced on its front page an experimental broadcast. The article referred to a "radio telephone" in one sentence and a "wireless telephone concert" in another. Pioneers of commercial radio weren't sure what to call it, but they could sense that it was big news.

Of course, no technology springs from a void. Physicists of the nineteenth century, working on ground sown centuries earlier by Isaac Newton, figured out that the universe is full of energy traveling in waves. Furthermore, humans experience this energy in different ways depending on the distance from one wave peak to the next—the "wavelength." Light is energy moving in tiny waves measuring in the billionths of a meter from peak to peak. Between roughly 390 billionths and 700 billionths lie all the visible colors and everything we see: every rainbow, every Rembrandt, every sunset, every lover's face. Even shorter waves, dubbed "X-rays," were found to have the power of making living skeletons and organs visible—though scientists such as Marie Curie also discovered, with tragic consequences, that such high-frequency radiation can be deadly.

Building on the work of earlier researchers, Guglielmo Marconi figured out how to use long waves, hundreds of meters from peak to peak, to carry information through the air. In 1895 the inventor successfully sent and received a Morse code message without using wires. The practical value of this innovation was soon obvious to the maritime industry. For the first time, ships could communicate even after they sailed out of sight. Charlie had grown up hearing the sensational story of Dr. Hawley Crippen. In 1910 the English physician poisoned his wife and set sail for Canada with his mistress. Scotland Yard broadcast an order for Crippen's arrest to the

Marconi operators aboard the ship, and when the vessel docked, the scoundrel was seized.

Even more dramatic: in 1912, when Charlie was six years old, Marconi operators stationed on the luxury steamship *Titanic* were credited with the rescue of more than seven hundred survivors of the great ship's wreck in the North Atlantic. The young men sent urgent SOS messages until their wireless machines failed as the ship sank.

By that time, other innovators had leapfrogged Marconi to begin sending voices and music via longwave energy. Their experiments advanced to the point that the U.S. government began licensing commercial radio stations in 1920. The federal Bureau of Standards, meanwhile, published instructions for building homemade crystal radio receivers. From a handful of stations at the beginning of 1922, the number of licensed broadcasters grew to nearly 600 stations nationwide just twelve months later.

One of the earliest licensed stations was WDAF, owned and operated by the *Star*. Newspapers were prominent pioneers in broadcasting, because they worried that radio might replace their print products. The "wireless telephone concert" announced in February was so successful that the Kansas City station began regular broadcasts around the time Charlie and his friends set out for California. When he returned home, Charlie built his first crystal radio set.

Once the airwaves opened, broadcasters had to fill them. The sheer novelty of radio might grab an audience, but it wouldn't hold listeners for long. WDAF struck early gold with daily reports on the ups and downs of commodity prices from the Kansas City Board of Trade—corn, wheat, pork, and so on. Farmers for a thousand miles in every direction tuned in for such vital information. Elsewhere, the radio station in Detroit covered a heavyweight prizefight, and sports broadcasting was born. An evangelist named Paul Rader delivered the first radio sermon, accompanied by a brass band, on Chicago's station. Still, something more was needed, and it came shortly after Charlie's return from the road, when radio met jazz.

It was a Friday night, September 22, 1922, a few weeks after Charlie's seventeenth birthday. The Board of Trade was closed for the weekend, so WDAF relocated its mobile broadcasting equipment to the downtown Newman Theater in Kansas City, the same place where Walt Disney's first short films had played a few months earlier. When the Newman wasn't showing movies, its big stage hosted vaudeville. On this night, the headliner was a local band called the Coon-Sanders Novelty Orchestra, a nine-piece combo led by the sweet-singing duo of drummer Carleton Coon and pianist Joe Sanders.

There were better musicians in town—most notably Bennie Moten and his Kansas City Orchestra, which launched such giants of jazz as Bill "Count" Basie, Jimmy Rushing, Ben Webster, and Walter Page. They would inspire a younger generation of Kansas City musicians that included Mary Lou Williams, Lester Young, and—most brilliant of them all—the dazzling and doomed Charlie "Bird" Parker. But the Coon-Sanders band was a group of white musicians playing for white audiences, and therefore safe for radio in this heyday of the Ku Klux Klan. The combo produced a danceable brand of jazz pumped up by an energetic tuba, thwacked and tickled by Coon on the drums, and hurried along by a strumming banjo.

Listeners loved what they heard. The show at the Newman was such a success that WDAF booked the Coon-Sanders orchestra as a nightly act, broadcasting live from the band's late set at the elegant Hotel Muehlebach. Announcer Leo Fitzpatrick was skeptical at first that anyone would listen to the midnight show beyond "a bunch of nighthawks." The nighthawks proved to be a numerous flock.

Riding the mostly clear airwaves to receivers as far away as Canada, the WDAF signal made fans wherever the band was heard. The crooning bandleaders renamed their combo the "Coon-Sanders Nighthawk Orchestra." As more and more listeners discovered the Nighthawks on their crystal sets, and a passion for late-night jazz bewitched the nation, Coon-Sanders became known as "the band that made radio famous." Stores soon filled with high-tech receivers, elaborate improvements over homemade crystal sets, with polished wooden cases and futuristic features like "filament rheostats" and "tickler dials." Kids begged their parents to let them stay up late enough to hear the band. The whole country seemed to know the words of an upbeat ditty—one of the first theme songs in broadcast history—written by Sanders, called "The Nighthawk Blues."

> When Coon and Sanders start to play
> Those Nighthawk Blues you start to sway;
> Tune right in on the radio
> Rat-a-tat-tat and say hello!
> From coast to coast and back again
> You can hear that syn-co-pated 'frain
> It's fair—to declare—
> Listen to the Nighthawk Blues!

Among those late-night devotees was Charlie White, now a high school graduate and man of the world. Like a lot of young people at that stage of life, he had a sense of where he wanted to go but wasn't sure how to get there. Tapping his toe to the Nighthawks under the eaves on the top floor of the Campbell Street house, Charlie had a realization. The popularity of the Nighthawks was creating a huge demand for up-tempo dance bands. If a couple of Kansas City boys could become radio's biggest stars, what was stopping Charlie? He could form a band, learn the Nighthawks' repertoire, and raise the money for college by playing jazz.

There was just one hitch: Charlie couldn't play an instrument. He never had patience for piano lessons. But musical talent ran in his family. His older sisters formed a popular trio act, and one of them became a full-fledged professional. In the era of silent films, prior to 1927, every movie theater had an organ or a piano as standard equipment, on which a musician improvised mood music to match the unfolding drama on-screen. Charlie's sister was one of Kansas City's best movie house musicians.

Charlie bought a used tenor saxophone from a high school buddy. The sale price included a brief tutorial in fingering and enough knowledge of the mouthpiece to make the thing honk. Charlie took it from there. As he listened to the Nighthawks, he breathed quietly into his saxophone, matching one note, then another. The notes added up until he was playing along.

Decades later, Charlie reflected: "When you don't have an income, you create. You find a job." Of course, it's not always so easy. Yet he put his finger on something important. Humans have more creativity, more possibility, than most of us ever touch. "Every child is an artist," Picasso observed. Charlie found the musical artist inside himself and gave that creature some air. The nightly broadcasts on WDAF were his apprenticeship. "I'd listen to Coon-Sanders at night and I'd try to play along with them," he said. "And I learned to play the sax. Never took a lesson."

In the meantime, he earned some cash at summer's end by working again as a railroad scab. Tensions remained high on picket lines, but Charlie hatched a plan to safely cross. He had a pair of natty white flannel trousers, such as a well-dressed office boy might wear to work. Garbed in flannels, he smuggled his laborer's overalls inside a book bag and passed unmolested through the line of strikers. "They'd say, 'Well, this kid is just working in the office,'" Charlie recalled. Once inside, he changed into the overalls, worked a shift, then hit the showers. "I'd put on my white flannel pants and walk out."

Charlie's railroad pay covered costs that fall at the new Junior College of Kansas City. I won't go into the history of junior colleges here. Trust me that this is another example of Charlie and the modern world coming of age together. For Charlie, junior college was an affordable way to get started toward his goal of becoming a doctor. And what this new option lacked in terms of grassy quads and bell towers, the junior college made up for in rigor. "It was the hardest school I ever went to. It was really tough," Charlie once told me. Perhaps the faculty felt they had something to prove. The students certainly felt that way. Charlie said the standards were so high, and the students so diligent, that when he later transferred to Missouri's flagship university, he found the work easy by comparison.

Every midnight, out came the saxophone for another practice session as a virtual sideman in the Nighthawk Orchestra. Charlie began lugging his sax around by day, ready to practice at any opportunity. He had a friend who was learning the banjo; now and then, on a warm evening, the pair would take the trolley to sprawling Swope Park, south of town, rent a canoe at the boathouse, and launch a floating jam session on the lagoon. Within a couple of years, Charlie had a repertoire of some three hundred songs.

Just as he envisioned it, he started making money. Charlie's pickup bands were a hit on the high school dance circuit. Kids would forgive a few wrong notes in exchange for energetic covers of popular tunes. In 1923, the smash hit was a sharply percussive number called "The Charleston," by the great African-American composer James P. Johnson. The tune produced a dance craze featuring a step invented in South Carolina, all knocking knees and swaying hips. But Charlie and the boys could also play a nice foxtrot and even a respectable waltz. They were good enough to score a weeklong engagement at the Mainstreet Theater downtown.

This was a grand time to be young in Kansas City. Dubbed "the Paris of the Plains" by the scandal-loving columnist Westbrook Pegler, the city was entering a wide-open, irrepressible age, fueled by thoroughgoing scorn for Prohibition. The Pendergast family, Irish immigrants from the stockyards, was sealing the grip of its political machine through targeted philanthropy, energetic election fraud, and the occasional murder. The expanse between Memphis and Chicago and points far to the west could be dry and prudish, but in the Kansas City of Boss Tom Pendergast, the party never stopped. "If you want to see some sin, forget about Paris and go to Kansas City," a visiting writer from Omaha would eventually declare, in the sort of exposé that worked wonders for tourism.

It was a place where big things happened quickly. Developer Jesse Clyde Nichols turned the rolling pig farms south of town into a planned community of grand mansions and upscale homes for the city's bankers, attorneys, merchants, garment makers, grain brokers, railroad operators, meatpackers, engineers, lumber barons, and factory owners. Nichols laid out winding streets and cul-de-sacs, golf courses and polo grounds. He built the nation's first pedestrian shopping mall, dubbed it the Country Club Plaza, and filled it with European statuary, burbling fountains, and a tower inspired by the Cathedral of Seville.

No African Americans were welcome in Nichols's narrow-minded neighborhoods, yet their community boomed as well. Drawn from farms in the South to join the Great Migration, descendants of the enslaved thrived on Kansas City's East Side. A former riverboat cook from Tennessee, Henry Perry, opened a smoked meat restaurant in an old trolley barn and gave birth to Kansas City's cult of barbecue. Nearby, in 1920, a group of entrepreneurs from across the country met at the East Side YMCA to organize a professional Negro baseball league, of which the Kansas City Monarchs quickly became a powerhouse. A person could stand at Eighteenth and Vine in those years and watch the who's who of African-American life pass by, for they all came to visit (and some came to live): pitcher Satchel Paige, contralto Marian Anderson, muralist Hale Woodruff, entrepreneur Effa Manley, author James Weldon Johnson, composer Duke Ellington. Roy Wilkins, the writer and political organizer destined to lead the NAACP through the civil rights movement, covered the scene as a young writer for the influential *Kansas City Call*.

Charlie's town was a way station between farm and future for countless young dreamers. The creator of Disneyland said he got his inspiration from Electric Park, the glittering amusement park south of downtown. Walt Disney was one of thousands of awestruck visitors who saw human tableaux emerge from splashing fountains on a magical hydraulic lift. He studied the carefully tended gardens framing the carnival rides, rode the miniature train that circled the grounds, and gaped as night became a fantasy of twinkling lights and bursting fireworks.

A teenager from eastern Nebraska, Joyce Clyde Hall, arrived at Union Station with two boxes of postcards to sell. Those two boxes became the greeting card and wrapping paper empire Hallmark. Another teenager, Nell Quinlan of rural Kansas, started sewing housedresses with a splash of style. Her company would become for many years the largest dressmaker in the world.

That was Kansas City after the Great War: the best of times and worst of times, you might say. A canvas for dreamers; a sty of corruption and the Klan. As Dickens wrote of revolutionary France—and really of all places and all times—the seasons of light and seasons of darkness were woven together in one eternal calendar, through which each person was challenged to find an honorable way of living. Charlie staked his future on the light, saying: "If you're negative, your whole body suffers. A negative person falls apart, because the food that is supplied with optimism is not present." An optimist does not deny darkness. Optimists like Charlie refuse to sink into it, to hide in it, to surrender to darkness.

A number of Charlie's high school friends were now students at the University of Kansas, in nearby Lawrence, to the west of Kansas City. Others had enrolled a few hours in the opposite direction at the University of Missouri. Faced with his own choice, Charlie visited the Phi Kappa Psi house at Kansas, where the brothers invited him to join them on a serenading tour of Sorority Row. Ninety years later, he still recalled the young women pointing and laughing as one of the singers paused to urinate in the bushes. (Even in "bone-dry" Kansas, home state of the anti-alcohol crusader Carry Nation, Prohibition was already a bust.) Ultimately, Charlie was influenced by a more sober example: his Sunday school chum Charles Parker, destined for a Rhodes scholarship at Missouri.

Parker was a member of the Beta Theta Pi fraternity, where Charlie joined the pledge class shortly after enrolling at Missouri in 1924. The worst of the hazing, he recalled long afterward, came when he and nineteen pledge brothers were ordered to extinguish a fire in the fireplace—by spitting water on it. Their water supply was up two flights of stairs. The pledges were required to duck-walk all the way. Up and down, up and down, up and down, with laughing upperclassmen pouring water into their mouths at the top of the stairs. "We finally put the fire out," Charlie remembered, "but the next day, none of us could go to class because we had waddled up and down those steps so long, our legs were just stiff."

He continued: "In Hell Week, fraternities, they paddled the guys. They did the most dire of dirty tricks. Anything devilish they could think of, they did to you. I remember they took me out at night about ten or fifteen miles out of town to a graveyard and said, 'You've got to find this guy's name and date of death.' They left me at about midnight. I had to wander all around this graveyard all by myself, looking at the grave markers to get this guy's name, and then walk back to town. I don't know. I guess it wasn't fifteen miles. It was probably only a mile out of town, but it seemed like fifteen miles to me."

Charlie loved life with the Betas as much as he loved his high school fraternity. And after the demands of junior college, he found university easy. His studies left plenty of time for music—he kept a textbook next to his chair while performing, and studied between sets—with time left over for carousing with friends.

Seasons of darkness: the same world that greeted Charlie could be fatally dangerous to African-Americans. A year before Charlie arrived at Missouri, a janitor on campus, accused of rape, was dragged from his jail cell by a drunken mob and lynched on a nearby bridge. Around the same time, a teacher in the sociology department was assailed for denying in a lecture that the theory of "pure races"—an intellectual antecedent of the Holocaust to come—was valid.

For Charlie, as for most students, such matters were a world away. He worried about lesser things, like the fact that there was no bridge connecting Columbia to the Kansas City side of the Missouri River. If a boisterous band of students roared off to the west in search of fun, they could easily miss the last ferryboat on their return. Charlie recalled skidding up to the crossing too late one night and sleeping in his car through a snowstorm.

After a carefree year at the university, Charlie was eligible to apply for Missouri's medical school. The process was a far cry from today's sequence of tests, applications, and interviews. Students with the required general education credits could apply for medical training as upper-level undergraduates. "You just sent in the paperwork," Charlie recalled.

The idea of being a doctor was planted at his mother's boardinghouse table, where Charlie was spellbound by the stories of the medical missionaries. His dream blossomed when one of his sisters married a doctor.

It's natural to look at a goal and think . . . it might not be attainable. The trick is to ignore the "not." Charlie had a gift for ignoring.

His education as a doctor came at the threshold of modern medicine, between the age of potions and the age of genome sequencing. To reach the future, medicine had to escape the reek of the past. Charlie learned before antibiotics, when the leading causes of death in America weren't heart disease and cancer. Those maladies kill mostly older people, and when Charlie was a student most people didn't grow old. Most people succumbed to the same viral and microbial illnesses that stalked humanity for ages—yet remained poorly understood and incurable. Childhood mortality was rampant, ending one in five lives in the United States before the age of five. Surgical treatments were rudimentary at best and rarely successful for long. The role of vitamins and hormones in human chemistry was only imagined, much less systematized.

The best-known doctor around Kansas City when Charlie was a student was Arthur Hertzler. Trained in pathology by leading European scientists, Hertzler founded a hospital near Wichita, practiced widely across rural Kansas, and traveled often to Kansas City to teach. Even Hertzler, this paragon of early-twentieth-century medical practice, described a disturbing helplessness in his memoir. A doctor's principal contribution, Hertzler wrote, was his demeanor. Having seen a lot of disease, the trained physician could distinguish patients likely to recover from patients likely to die soon. A doctor's bedside manner could help patients and families speed recovery or prepare for the inevitable. But as for answering the ravages of illness: "I can scarcely think of a single disease that the doctors actually cured during those early years," Hertzler wrote. "Doctors knew how to relieve suffering, set bones, sew up cuts and open boils on small boys."

In the absence of cures, sick people sought out quacks and frauds. In many respects, the field of medicine when Charlie entered it was a circus of flamboyant incompetence. Newspapers of the 1920s and '30s carried "news articles" virtually indistinguishable from actual journalism in tone or appearance, which were actually advertisements for unregulated tonics packed with alcohol or narcotics. These addictive elixirs purported to treat maladies ranging from hair loss to cancer, gout to gonorrhea, flatulence to heart disease.

The most spectacular charlatans married malpractice with mass communication, and they thrived in the Midwest, like soybeans and walleye. E. Virgil Neal of Sedalia, Missouri, for instance. Neal built a mail-order empire peddling pills to increase height, enhance bust size, and vanquish all sorts of undiagnosed complaints. His miracle ingredient he called "nuxated iron" (the "nux" involved traces of highly poisonous strychnine), and he pioneered celebrity athlete endorsements. Baseball's Ty Cobb and boxer Jack Dempsey touted the powers of nuxated iron.

Norman Baker of Muscatine, Iowa, was another great charlatan. After launching his own radio station in 1925, Baker brewed a toxic blend of conspiracy theories and patent medicines—turpentine for lockjaw, onion poultices for appendicitis, and a mysterious powder for brain tumors. He insisted that licensed doctors were corrupt. Pediatricians were child molesters, Baker preached over the airwaves. "M.D." stood for "more dough."

In 1929, Baker came across the work of Dr. Charles Ozias of Kansas City, who had concocted a secret serum that he promised would cure cancer if injected into tumors. Baker touted the cure on his radio show and soon was operating a one-hundred-bed cancer clinic. He touted another "cure" as well, cooked up by Harry Hoxsey of Illinois from an old family recipe. Pressed about his formulas in a court proceeding, Baker acknowledged that he brewed clover, corn silk, and watermelon seed in water, just as Hoxsey advised.

Baker eventually relocated with his hospital, his radio audience, and his watermelon seeds to a looming Victorian hotel on a hilltop in the spa town of Eureka Springs, Arkansas. He painted the lobby purple to match his limousine and outfitted his office with bullet-proof glass. One wing of the hotel was insulated with soundproof-ing so that new patients could not hear the agonized moans of the defrauded dying.

A still greater quack—and bigger celebrity—was John Romulus Brinkley, who operated a radio station and clinic in Milford, Kansas. Licensed in "eclectic medicine" (whatever that was), Brinkley took cures wherever he found them: forgotten folklore, herbal brews, borrowings from chiropractors, osteopaths, homeopaths, and more exotic healers. His signature breakthrough was the idea of trans-planting goat testes into impotent men. "A man is only as old as his glands," Brinkley maintained.

He built a huge following—among the largest radio audiences in the nation—by interspersing pitches for his "Goat Gland Cure" with fundamentalist sermons, rants against elites, and bedtime sto-ries for kids. Tiny Milford filled with men from across the country willing to pay $750 each for goat testicle implants. The numbers grew as Brinkley "discovered" further applications for his interspe-cies transplants. Goat gonads supposedly cured diabetes, high blood pressure, epilepsy, deafness, paralysis, female infertility, obesity, and dementia.

Both Baker and Brinkley were targeted by the American Medical Association—Brinkley called the doctors' organization the "Amal-

gamated Meatcutters Association." Hounded from the United States
in the 1930s, they set up new radio stations, ten times more powerful than U.S. law would permit, in the border town of Villa Acuna,
Mexico. Wire fences in the area hummed from the powerful signals.
Reputedly earning millions per year in the depths of the Depression,
neither man could resist returning to the United States to seek public office. Norman Baker lost his bid for a U.S. Senate seat in Iowa,
and Brinkley fell short in his campaign for governor of Kansas.

This was the wild frontier of quackery that Charlie's medical education was intended to tame. But when I had a chance to examine
Charlie's well-preserved class notes, I was struck by how meager
an arsenal he was given. Medical students of the 1920s memorized
the names and symptoms of hundreds of ailments and disorders,
but the treatments they learned were almost never equal to the
diseases. Whether he was studying wounds and tuberculosis with
Dr. Buchbinder, surgery with Dr. Shrager, or neurology with Dr.
Pollock; whether the subject was syphilis or snakebite, nasal tumors
or diarrhea, the weak link was always the same: no cures.

For instance, Charlie learned the following possible therapies for
gonorrhea: silver nitrate ointment, intravenous injections of mer-
curochrome, intramuscular injections of sterile milk, and prostate
massage. Removing the tonsils was advised as a treatment for "rheu-
matism, heart disease, joint, eye, ear, kidney + [gastrointestinal] diseases, etc.," Charlie noted dutifully. Cocaine in a spray solution was
recommended for the common cold. No wonder so many patients
were susceptible to the blandishments of radio healers spinning conspiracy theories about doctors conniving to keep patients sick. "All
we could really do is sit by our patients and pray," Charlie admitted
long afterward.

Not that Charlie was particularly pastoral. His anatomy teacher was Edgar Allen, a celebrated biochemist who had etched his name into medical history by isolating the female hormone estrogen and documenting its effects. Students were awed by Allen's accomplishments, and by his skill as a sailboat skipper. Yet even Allen's reputation was not enough to tame Charlie's appetite for mischief. "One night," Charlie recalled, "we took one of the monkey cadavers that he used for his estrogen studies. We cooked that monkey's brain and we each had a taste." After a brief pause for reflection, Charlie added: "Medical students were a wild and unpredictable bunch in those days."

The capstone to his undergraduate education was Dr. Marcus Pinson Neal's grueling pathology course, which began for Charlie on February 1, 1927. Neal was a soft-spoken southerner, raised in Alabama and educated in Virginia, with a long, patrician face and small, steel-rimmed glasses. Charlie arrived in class with about two hundred fresh pages of narrow-lined notebook paper clipped into his canvas-covered binder, and no sooner was he seated than his pen was racing to keep up. According to Charlie's notebook headings, Neal began with the "History and Definition" of pathology—the study of disease—and soon was ripping through "Etiology, Circulatory changes, retrograde changes, Anomalies and abnormalities, Inflammation, Poisons, Sudden Deaths, Infectious Diseases, General diseases, Tumors, blood-forming organs, the circulatory system, lymph nodes, the spleen, the respiratory system, the digestive system, the pancreas, the liver, the urinary organs, male reproductive organs, female reproductive organs, muscles, bones, joints and the nervous system"—all leading in four blistering months to a crushing final exam.

In neat, careful script, covering each notebook page front and back, Charlie compiled nearly four hundred pages of detailed notes describing the symptoms, treatments, and prognoses of every known disease and injury. Neal explained how to take a patient history. He counseled the proper manner of conducting a general exam (with particular attention to performing a rectal examination on a "typical nervous patient").

Charlie learned how to treat wounds. ("In greasy wound use turpentine or gasoline to remove grease + act as sterilizing agent.") He learned to lance and drain boils, and how to surgically remove the boil's more dangerous cousin, the carbuncle. For infections, he was taught to prescribe "heliotherapy"—that is, sunshine—and for thrombosis he learned to order an "absolutely quiet" month in bed. Charlie learned to give coffee to patients in shock and opium suppositories to patients with hemorrhoids. Mercury, a highly toxic element, was the treatment of choice for a wide range of diseases. Charlie and his fellow aspiring general practitioners were encouraged to experiment with immunology by stirring up "autogenous vaccines" for a variety of ailments. The method was not complicated, nor was it very effective. The future doctors were taught to extract infected matter from a diseased organ or wound, then mix it in solution. The finished soup was injected back into the patient in hopes of stimulating the immune response.

Week after grueling week, Charlie absorbed the insights as well as the mistakes and blind spots of his chosen profession. When Professor Neal completed his last lecture, Charlie went painstakingly through the notebook, preparing for the final. Ultimately his canvas-backed book was a compendium for the general practitioner of the late 1920s; it contained at least a half-baked nostrum for every medical condition he was likely to see, from constipation to cancer to the clap; from broken bones to tuberculosis to infant jaundice.

He paid his bills with a small stipend from home and the money he made with his saxophone. "I was busy every Friday and Saturday," he recalled of the endless student dances. "Even Friday afternoons, I played tea dances at sororities and all. I guess I knew everybody in the Greek section of school—sororities and fraternities, you knew them all because you played their parties, you know."

In a quintessential Charlie coda, he added: "It was a great life."

On Commencement Day, 1927, Charlie received his undergraduate degree in medicine from the University of Missouri. He was twenty-one years old. For reasons lost to time, his mother was unable to attend the ceremony. Instead she sent a letter.

There is a lot that I came to admire about Laura White. Her world was shattered by her husband's early death, yet she found the resolve to support her large family. Charlie adored her. Little time went by in our friendship before Charlie told me proudly that she was named "Mother of the Year" for her skill at balancing work, faith, and parenting. By today's standards, though, she could seem almost neglectful. In Charlie's memory, her parenting boiled down to a single all-purpose piece of advice: "Just do the right thing." The simplicity is so removed from my own generation of helicopter parents. My parenting mistakes (and I've made plenty) stem from overinvolvement rather than benign neglect.

Laura White's faith in her son to do the right thing, and her trust in his resourcefulness, powerfully nourished his confidence. I can see that now. Children need room to make their own choices, learn their own lessons, suffer their own consequences, and dust themselves off. Perhaps the most difficult lesson for today's supremely protective parents: Laura White raised her son as if the world were a mostly safe and manageable place. She did this in spite of the freak violence that killed her husband. Through her, Charlie absorbed a faith that things would come out well.

I understood this better after Charlie died. Among his things was the letter Laura sent for his graduation day, in which she strove to be mother and dad to a young man who needed both. She wrote:

> *My blessed boy.*
>
> *I just feel I must send you a little love letter on this your graduation day, as I cannot be with you in person. I'm sure you know mother's deepest love and lovingest thoughts are with you, and this is a proud and happy day for her. I've been thinking how proud your own father would have been on this day in your life. He always said you should have college training and I believe you know, dear, that along with my own hopes and dreams for you, I have carried in my heart his wishes that you might be equipped to make the best of your life. He had great ideals and ambitions for his sonny boy, and it is said, any good father wants his son to become the man he hoped to be. You were the pride of his life from the time the nurse placed you in his arms, until his going away.*
>
> *My prayer has been—and his, dear heart—that you live, play the game, and so work out the days of your life that will bring fulfillment to you and all who love you, and believe in you. You have chosen a noble profession, a high road of service, and will be true to its finest traditions. Remember in every profession as in*

every life: There is a high road and a low road, and some will take the high road and some will take the low road, and in between, in the misty flaps the rest drift to and fro.

The deepest feelings of the heart are difficult to express, but I'm sure you know I love you, believe in you, have joy in you, pray for the best to come to you that is for your own best good. And thank God for giving me such a dear, dear son. This may not be a red-letter day to you, but in retrospect it will become so, more and more.

Charlie treasured those sentences for eighty-seven years. He often mentioned their unusually warm tone as the decades wore on. The letter was nearby when he breathed his last. His mother believed in him, had joy in him, and Charlie had taken the high road, as she had hoped.

He played the game.

seven

Charlie was somewhere between boyhood and manhood, on the strange frontier of adolescence, when Lyle Willits started coming around the Campbell Street house to court Charlie's oldest sister. There was something quite winning about Willits, because Charlie's sister was not the only one to fall under the spell of his charm. So did Charlie.

Willits was nine years older than Charlie, at a time in life when nine years is everything, especially to a fatherless boy in need of footsteps to follow. The importance of this friendship and role modeling can be seen in the fact that Charlie began to build his future on the blueprint of his oldest brother-in-law. Willits was a young doctor, which made Charlie believe he could be a doctor, too. Willits was a graduate of the medical school at Northwestern University in Chicago. So, as his undergraduate career approached its end, Charlie also set his sights on Northwestern. To his dismay, Northwestern turned Charlie down.

What happened next was pure Charlie White. His rejection was a hard blow, but it did not leave him powerless. The disappointment could be turned into a challenge, a chance to test his own strength. He boarded a train for Chicago, found his way to Evanston, and located the office of the medical school dean. Though he had no appointment, Charlie announced himself at the desk and sat down to wait until the dean would see him.

I picture the baffled look on the dean's face when his assistant informed him that a persistent young man from Missouri had planted himself in the waiting room. Evidently, curiosity got the better of the man, because Charlie was ushered into the dean's office. Talking fast, Charlie explained why turning him away was a mistake. Perhaps Lyle Willits gave him a pep talk, encouraging Charlie to feel that he was up to the rigors of Northwestern. Certainly he went armed with his record at Missouri as evidence of his study habits. Whatever Charlie said, it worked. He talked his way in.

My kids and I have argued on this score. They tell me that no one gets ahead through face-to-face contacts anymore. Job hunting, networking, and the pursuit of opportunity all happen online. You fill out an electronic form, post a digital resume, click the button, and accept your fate. But I'm not sure I believe it. Technology changes, but people don't. The human touch will always matter. An earnest young person confidently making a case is as powerful today as a century ago. Maybe it is no longer possible to talk your way into an elite medical school. But you can still be your own best advocate. No one else can do it as well. As for the risk of rejection—Charlie had already been rejected. His trip to the dean's office offered only upside.

There's a true story about Kris Kristofferson, the singer and actor who wound up in the songwriting hall of fame. When he came home from Vietnam as a young man, he had nothing but his training as a helicopter pilot and a strong faith in himself. He believed the songs he was writing were worthy of attention, yet the world refused to notice. He borrowed a chopper, flew to the outskirts of Nashville, and landed on the lawn of superstar Johnny Cash. When Cash came out to see what was happening, Kristofferson handed him a tape of his songs.

That was in the spirit of Charlie White.

My own Charlie moment came when I was seventeen years old. I heard about a job typing box scores and writing brief stories on weekend nights in the sports department of my local newspaper, the *Denver Post*. Calling the sports editor to ask for an interview was the hardest thing I had ever done. I was terrified. The telephone hung on the wall in our kitchen, with the receiver attached by a long curlicue cord. When I lifted the receiver to place the call, it felt like it weighed four hundred pounds. Every digit I dialed into the phone was another invitation to give up.

A gruff voice answered, and I could barely get a word from my constricted throat. After the editor brushed me off—a high school kid asking for a job at a big-city newspaper!   calling him back again a few days later was even harder. Calling the third time was sheer torture. But the third call got me an interview, and the interview got me the job, and the job led to my career.

Disappointment is one of those external things beyond a person's control and therefore, to a Stoic, unworthy of attention. Charlie could control his response to disappointment, though. He chose to persist. He could make a better case for himself than his application alone had done. So he took the risk of further disappointment in pursuit of the reward he sought. And there came a day in 1927 when

Charlie White entered the Northwestern University medical school, all of twenty-two years old, and immediately set to work delivering on his promises to the dean.

Everything Charlie told the man turned out to be correct: Charlie was smart enough, worked hard enough, and mixed so easily with his classmates that the dean never had reason to regret his decision. The proof was in Charlie's first-year grades. In obstetrics, the medical art of safely delivering babies (and related matters of reproductive health): A-minus.

Medical jurisprudence: A-minus.

Neurology: A-minus.

Pediatrics: B. Dermatology: B. And so on. Initially denied admission, Charlie wound up far above the class average.

By now the Roaring Twenties were in full roar, and every Friday and Saturday night Charlie could be found with his saxophone on a bandstand somewhere around the Windy City. His musical inspirations, the Coon-Sanders Nighthawks, had moved their base of operations to Chicago, where the band was known to be a favorite of the gangster boss Al Capone. Charlie continued to study his textbooks between sets.

He also grabbed shifts as a city ambulance attendant to make extra money—the 1920s version of today's EMTs. One wild night in Capone's Chicago, his ambulance was called to the scene of a gangland shoot-out. A mobster lay on the sidewalk with a severe case of lead poisoning. The man's female companion was distraught and pleaded with Charlie to do something. When the doctor-in-training knelt beside the fallen gangster and checked his fluttering pulse, it was obvious that there was no hope. A spreading pool of crimson told the tale.

"He can't survive without a transfusion," Charlie announced—though in those days you could fit everything known to physicians about the infant science of blood transfusion onto a couple of index cards with room left for a grocery list. Sometimes a transfusion worked. Other times the new blood seemed to cause a toxic reaction. Researchers were still figuring out the details of blood typing.

The gangster's girlfriend offered to pay handsomely for last-ditch heroics. So, digging into the ambulance supplies, Charlie produced a length of rubber tubing and two IV needles. Plunging one needle into his own arm and the other into the arm of the dying man, Charlie and the moll watched as the rubber tube filled with Charlie's blood. Whether the patient and his would-be healer had compatible blood types would never be known, because the rash experiment failed to save the wounded man.

But the bereaved girlfriend was moved by the attempt and, true to her word, she produced a wad of cash from which she peeled a generous sum and pressed the bills into Charlie's hand.

This was fortuitous, for he had a use for the money already in mind. With the summer holiday approaching, Charlie had recently visited the Chicago office of a trans-Pacific cruise ship line with an offer to supply a dance band for their next cruise across the Pacific. The offer was accepted, and Charlie had no trouble finding musicians willing to spend the summer sailing from Seattle to Japan, on to China, and back. The wages were small, but the passage was free and the food abundant. Better yet: passengers were known to pass the hat to tip the band at the end of each voyage.

Only after the gig was finalized did Charlie focus on one loose end: train fare from Chicago to Seattle. Now, like an answered prayer, he held a wad of money still warm from the hand of a dead man's girlfriend. It was more than enough to cover his trip.

⌒⌒

Charlie kept a diary of that voyage, and it was still among his things when he died more than eighty-five years later. Before he set out, he wrote down the lyrics to a couple of dozen of songs that he liked—mostly slow and sentimental ones—in the first pages. This prompt book was a compilation of tunes popular on the radio and as 78-rpm wax records. I imagine he wanted a handy list of tunes his band could play and sing should audience requests falter. "Little Log Cabin of Dreams" was the latest hit from bandleader Paul Whiteman. "Nobody's Sweetheart" was everybody's favorite, covered by one band after another. "Russian Lullaby" was a dreamy waltz fresh from the genius of Irving Berlin. And so on.

Later pages, marked with the dates of summer, strained to hold Charlie's record of the grand adventure: each formal supper, afternoon tea dance, and Sunday brunch the band played. For the first week or so at sea, Charlie listed every mouthful of food from the ship's cornucopia—until a storm stirred a few days of wallowing waves and seasickness extinguished his passion for the menu. After that he spent more time between dances in his bunk, plowing through a popular novel by the British writer Philip Gibbs, called *Young Anarchy*.

Published a year after *The Great Gatsby*, and touching on some of the same themes of lost roots and disrupted morals, the book struck a note of pessimism that would recur in Western culture several times throughout Charlie's long life. Young people had lost their moorings. Values and virtues were a thing of the past. The world was well on its way to hell in a handbasket. The author of *Gatsby* once spoke of Charlie's "generation grown up to find all Gods dead, all wars fought, all faiths in man shaken." Gibbs, in *Young Anarchy*, described a similar crisis of confidence: something "smashed . . . in the minds of men—age-old traditions of thought, the foundations of faith, many hopes and illusions in the soul of humanity, the ancient discipline of social life."

When I leafed through his well-preserved diary, Charlie's hours in the bunk with the Gibbs novel grabbed my attention. My kids, just like Charlie, have come of age in a period of disillusionment and pessimism. As dark as things seem in the 2020s, they aren't any darker than the 1920s. Charlie had the right reaction, I believe. He enjoyed the novel even though he could not embrace the author's dark outlook. Throughout his life, Charlie never imagined things to be any worse—or any better—than they really were, for he had learned at an early age that life is never as sure as we might think, nor as hopeless as it might appear.

The ship docked in bustling Yokohama, Japan, where Charlie and his pals saw the damage left by a recent catastrophic earthquake. Onward it sailed to Manila, where Charlie watched with delight as five cocky young men from Yale failed to "accomplish much" with the young women on the dance floor. A terrible cold settled into Charlie's chest and sinuses as the ship reached Hong Kong. By the end of August, the voyagers were back in Honolulu, still playing their regular performances and gladly accepting tips from passengers at each terminal port. By then Charlie was in a hurry to get home for a brief stop in Kansas City on his way back to his final year of medical school.

The cruise to China was a glorious trip, one that broadened Charlie's horizons. But I don't think it changed his life. The Asia adventure was another version of his California odyssey in the Model T. A more sheltered young man turning twenty-three might have needed to have his eyes opened, but Charlie, by then, was fully alert and alive.

He had decided many years earlier how he would face the world. As a boy, he began narrating a story about himself to himself, a story of pluck and success, and he acted on that premise until it came true. He understood that, whether we sail to a new continent or simply travel from one day to the next, we are always headed into the unknown. Charlie had learned to treat the unknown as a friend, until life convinced him otherwise. Though he lived to an extraordinary age, it never did.

Experience shapes us. And we shape our experiences by turning them into our life stories. We give them their meaning. As the poet E. E. Cummings, whose star was ascendant in the late 1920s, wrote, "Once we believe in ourselves we can risk curiosity, wonder, spontaneous delight, or any experience that reveals the human spirit."

Once we believe . . .

After Northwestern, he looked homeward for his internship—the last step between Charlie and his goal of becoming a doctor. Lyle Willits encouraged Charlie to pursue an opening at Kansas City General Hospital, among the first institutions in the nation to guarantee care regardless of a patient's ability to pay. The huge brick-and-limestone edifice stood on a hill about a mile from the house on Campbell Street; Charlie must have passed it many times on his way to and from downtown. Yet, as he walked through the doors for the first time as a healer, he might have noticed with fresh eyes the lines from Shakespeare incised in the stone overhead: "The Quality of Mercy is not strained, it droppeth as the gentle rain from heaven upon the place beneath."

Built at a cost of some half a million dollars around the time Charlie was born, Kansas City General boasted such up-to-date facilities as an ice-making plant and a separate wing for infectious children. (Another friend I made in Kansas City told me of her struggle for life as a young girl sick with meningitis in that isolation wing. It was a desperately lonely story.)

The hospital accepted all comers and treated most of the city's urgent cases. It was, Charlie recalled, the only hospital in the city equipped to handle emergencies. Adding to the excitement for a doctor-in-training, General Hospital interns served on the city's ambulances. Between work in the hospital and around the city, interns were so busy that the hospital maintained a dormitory for them on the fifth floor; they literally lived their work. And there was no easing into it. General Hospital interns were tossed into the deep end of the medical pool, to sink or swim. "We were given a lot of responsibility to do things," Charlie remembered happily, adding, "if we could handle them."

As the public hospital of a booming city, General Hospital treated every variety of disease and injury. Charlie was in a hurry to see and experience it all, from the surgery suite for "unclean cases" to the quarantine rooms for victims of seasonal epidemics; from the maternity ward to the emergency room, where rough men arrived wounded by bullets or razors.

He often told a story that captured his impatience to learn: With his fellow interns, Charlie was summoned to a surgery suite by Dr. Underwood one Saturday morning to learn the all-important technique of clipping out tonsils. Like all doctors of his era, Charlie had been taught that a long list of ailments had tonsil-related causes. Removing the tiny organs in the throat was believed to be a reset button on human health. So there was no more practical lesson than the one they were about to receive.

But when the interns gathered to absorb this information, Dr. Underwood announced with regret that the patient had failed to appear as scheduled. The excitement drained from the room. Then Charlie piped up: "I still have mine," he said. For a moment, the surgeon seemed not to understand.

"You can take out my tonsils," Charlie volunteered, removing his coat and loosening his collar. Climbing onto the operating table, Charlie settled into position as a mirror was found. He watched the surgery in the mirror as his fellow interns crowded around his open mouth. "That's the kind of life we lived. We didn't worry about crazy things," said Charlie—delighted to see in my face just how crazy such things sounded.

"Most of the time," he continued, the interns were even more spontaneous, and even less supervised. "We just went ahead and did things on our own," he reported. "And most of the time, we got away with it all right." He loved telling the story of a patient who arrived at the hospital with his arm dangling limply from a dislocated shoulder joint.

The diagnosis was easy. But none of the interns had ever reconnected a dislocated shoulder. They anesthetized the man with ether, then went to work. "We couldn't get it reduced," Charlie recalled, using the lingo of doctors that means putting the pieces of an injury back into place. "All three of us tried, and we couldn't." The arm dangled stubbornly.

Swallowing their pride, the young men summoned the hospital's attending physician. "He came right away. He looked at us. The patient was still asleep. He slipped it right in, and it looked so easy, and he left."

The interns exchanged glances. They eyed the patient, still dozing without feeling. "We looked back at each other and said: You know, we can do it now."

So Charlie and the others decided to try the maneuver again. They popped the shoulder out of the socket. The tranquilized patient slept on. "We tried and tried and tried, and we couldn't get it back in the second time," Charlie recalled. No matter how they jimmied the limb, they couldn't duplicate the effortless motion of the veteran doctor. Defeated, the interns summoned the older man again.

"He came and slipped it back in," Charlie recounted. And the interns finally discovered the limit of their free run of the hospital. "He looked at all three of us and said: 'Now, boys, leave this man alone.'"

Eventually each intern was assigned to a month of solo house calls. Patients around the city, too sick or otherwise unable to come in to the hospital, would call the switchboard to ask for a doctor. The intern on "service" was given an automobile (called a "sick car") and a driver who knew every dip and turn of the city. With a bag full of instruments and such rudimentary medicines as were available, Charlie set off each morning on the first of what would be twenty or twenty-five calls by the end of a long day. Then back again the next day. "It was a good learning experience," he reflected. For example, Charlie learned to differentiate between a ruptured appendix and a painful kidney stone, to call an ambulance for the first, and to prescribe aspirin, fluids, and plenty of courage for the second.

Most of all, he learned humility, for he quickly discovered how little his medical training had to offer for most patients. Charlie could drain a painful boil, salve a topical burn, stitch up an ugly gash. But the truth was, most of what he diagnosed he could not cure. Antibiotics and other advanced medicines had not been discovered. A crude X-ray was the forward edge of internal imaging. Charlie set fractures by feel, without ever seeing the bones beneath the skin. And he set a lot of them, because people were still routinely breaking their arms, wrists, or hands when their hand-cranked automobiles backfired. He carried bandages and plaster in his bag to make protective casts.

He went forth armored in the theory of "counter-irritation." To fight an infection, the theory said, a doctor should provoke the immune system. A favored technique was the mustard plaster. From the kitchen of a patient's home, the visiting intern combined dry mustard and flour, mixed the powder with warm water into a paste, and spread the paste over the patient's chest. Did it help? It was the best they had.

Charlie harbored no illusions. The most a doctor could offer, he soon concluded, was the reassurance that with bed rest, proper nutrition, and plenty of fluids, nature would gradually work a cure in most cases. "It was mostly supportive care—supporting them and trying to make them comfortable while the body healed itself," Charlie said.

The interns also served a public health function, in hopes of preventing disease if they could not cure it. While visiting private homes they gave tips on nutritious diets and made suggestions for proper hygiene and sanitation. Charlie and his colleagues were free with their opinions because lawsuits against doctors were virtually unheard-of, and medical insurance was mostly unknown. Even brand-new doctors were rarely second-guessed—although it did not take Charlie long to realize that in a field where trust was the strongest medicine, he was at a deficit. "People would look at me with a little doubt in their eyes. I looked so young! 'Are you a doctor?' they asked." In hopes of appearing older, he grew the mustache he would wear for nearly ninety years.

After taking his turn in the sick car, Charlie returned to riding the hospital's ambulances when they were called to emergencies. On the wild streets of Kansas City, traveling by ambulance was a high-stakes thrill. "These drivers were crazy," Charlie said.

Years later, he remembered one particularly wild ride involving an intrusive, self-inviting passenger. "There was a reporter for the *Star* who would hang around and go out on every call that might make a story," he explained. "He was sort of an obnoxious guy. One call, I took care of the patient at the scene and there was no need to bring them back to the hospital. So this reporter said, 'Well, the cot's empty. I'm going to lie down while we go back.'

"Those ambulance drivers always went fast. The doors opened on the side, not in the back like they do now. When we made the turn at Thirty-First and Troost Avenue, it felt like we went up on two wheels. The doors flew open. The cot rolled right out onto the street with this reporter on it."

For a year, the hospital was Charlie's whole life; his mother might as well have lived a hundred miles away. General Hospital even supplied his thoughts of love. There he met an attractive teenager working on one of the wards, Mildred Christel. Something sparked between them, and when Charlie had rare free time, he asked her on a date. The attraction was mutual.

Though Charlie was a marvelous storyteller, I don't recall any mention of serious girlfriends before Mildred. I formed a sense, perhaps wrong, that he may have been late to love. After all, he grew up two years younger than his classmates, still a child when the older boys were sprouting whiskers and turning to romance. He spent his college date nights up on the bandstand, playing his saxophone rather than snuggling close for a dance and a kiss. Whatever his level of experience might have been, the match with Mildred was something different, and they were married as soon as his internship ended.

There he was at last: Dr. Charles White! But there was a catch, he quickly discovered. Unlike most medical schools at the time, Northwestern did not allow its graduates to take the licensing exam as interns. When Charlie completed his internship, he was too late to sign up for the test. He would have to wait another year, until the next round of exams, before he could have his license. "I just wanted to practice medicine," he recalled, the desperation still in his voice many decades later. "But I missed the time to apply for state boards."

Rules are rules. The rules said Charlie needed his MD degree to qualify for the exams. Northwestern's rules said he could not get the degree until he completed his internship. Other schools had different rules, but this rule governed Charlie's options—or so it seemed. Of course, Charlie was not going to surrender meekly to the obstacles. There was nothing stopping him from finding the person in charge of licenses and respectfully making his case.

He set out for the state capital, Jefferson City. "I went down to talk to the state board, the doctor who was head of it." Charlie painted the whole picture for the man: his rigorous undergraduate studies at the University of Missouri, his excellent medical school preparation at Northwestern, his wide-ranging internship at Kansas City's busy General Hospital. He explained the flukes of bad timing that Northwestern's rules had impressed on his fledgling career. He threw himself on the mercy of the state licensing board.

But rules were rules. Charlie would have to wait until next year.

The board chairman liked what he saw in Charlie, however, and he offered a practical suggestion—one that would not do for a timid soul but worked perfectly well for Charlie. "He said: 'Son, you went to a good medical school, and you had a good internship. Just go on and practice.' So I practiced medicine for a year without a license," Charlie recalled matter-of-factly. Once again, he placed a bet on himself and the bet paid off.

As he promised he would do if Charlie came back to Kansas City, Lyle Willits gave him a little space in his clinic and "threw me a few cases." But Charlie was mostly on his own to find patients to support a new doctor and his newlywed wife. He received some referrals from the doctors at General Hospital who were impressed by Charlie's work as an intern. With time, he added patients by word of mouth. But building a practice was slow going.

During their courtship, Charlie and Mildred surely spent some of their rare free evenings strolling the sidewalks of the new Country Club Plaza. This fantasy of Spanish-style architecture, with its wide sidewalks and imported fountains, was a triumph of the City Beautiful movement, a nationwide campaign to redeem the choked and muddy boomtowns of the nineteenth century with landscaped parks, leafy boulevards, monumental buildings, and banks of flower beds. Led by the local newspaper editor William Rockhill Nelson,

Kansas City embraced the movement with such enthusiasm that eventually it would claim to have more fountains than any city in the world apart from Rome. Country Club Plaza took shape on land that had previously been pig farms, and was the nation's first planned shopping center outside a central business district. Accessible by car, it was really intended for pedestrians to promenade and window-shop. Young lovers on tight budgets like Charlie and Mildred could pass an evening strolling and laughing, with a pause at the bowling alley, perhaps, or for an ice cream cone.

Nearby, across a flood-prone stream called Brush Creek, Charlie could not help but notice an elegant nine-story apartment building of red brick with Italianate towers and stone accents. The developer intended to evoke the magnificent buildings lining Central Park in Manhattan; whether the goal was achieved or not, the Villa Serena was an emphatic statement in 1920s Kansas City. Another brother-in-law was involved somehow in the project; his wedding gift to Charlie and Mildred was several months of free rent at Villa Serena, with its magnificent lobby, hair salon, complimentary maid service, and Hotpoint appliances. (No air-conditioning, though. Charlie often spoke of the hot, humid nights of long-ago summers, when he and many other residents carried cots to the roof of the apartment building to sleep outside.)

Wary of taking on a rent obligation that he wouldn't be able to meet, Charlie chose the smallest available studio unit. Then he suggested to management that they add another amenity: a house physician, on-call after hours. To Charlie, the Villa Serena wasn't just a swell place to live; it was a potential hive of new patients. Management happily accepted his offer.

It's not right to say that Charlie was finally on his own. He had been on his own a long time: when he darted from a train and walked the last miles home from a pedophile's summer camp as an eight-year-old; when he drove halfway across the country on rutted roads and surfed freight trains home at sixteen; when he made himself a musician by listening to the radio and turned that little career into a college education and a voyage halfway around the world; when he delivered babies and watched patients die and pumped his own blood into a Chicago gangster. I came to think that Charlie's gift was his natural understanding and embrace of the existential idea that we're always on our own. We ask, we learn, we take counsel, we emulate, but when we finally act, it's *our* action.

Even if we aren't "on our own," we might as well think and behave as though we are. I'm not talking about selfishness or narcissism or alienation. I am talking about acting as if we are free to make good choices instead of bad ones. We are "on our own" in the sense of having power to sacrifice, to love, to forgive. Charlie, I think, had a natural perception that every life meets obstacles and setbacks, some more difficult than others and some more unjust. But there is always some scope of self-determination, no matter how narrow. In that space, we are on our own.

Of course, the more common meaning refers to the time when a person crosses the invisible line between youth and adulthood. We say: He's on his own. She's on her own. A career begins, a home is made, perhaps a spouse is wed. This was Charlie at age twenty-five in 1930. He was a doctor with a scraggly mustache—house doctor at the glamorous Villa Serena. He had a very young wife and a tiny apartment in a grand building. He was on his own . . . and then the whole world turned against him.

Look at the calendar: 1930.

Despite what we may have learned in history class, the stock market crash of 1929 was not a one-day affair. The market flapped and struggled through the autumn of 1929 as Charlie neared the end of his internship. It plunged in late October, before beating its wings as if to fly again. As Charlie launched his career, many people remained hopeful that the crash was just a brief interlude on the way to the next boom. A "correction," as optimistic brokers like to say.

But it was no correction. Almost half the yearly industrial production of the United States was wiped out by 1933. The gross national product dropped by one-third. Unemployment rose past 20 percent. The Depression would loom over Charlie's career like an angry, stifling cloud for more than ten years. Born around 1905, his generation was too young to have made much money in the Roaring Twenties. But the Depression cost them dearly in terms of lost years and career struggles.

During one of my visits across the street, we were talking— I should say, Charlie was talking; I was listening in amazement— about the cost of medical care in the early 1930s, when Charlie was getting started. He recalled the rates immediately: two dollars to visit the doctor's office, three dollars for a house call, five dollars for a house call after hours. But he realized how misleading this was. Most bills weren't paid, he said. He could ask for a million dollars, but how much could he actually get? "In the real heart of the big Depression," Charlie said, "a nickel car fare was not available" to many Kansas City families. What difference did it make if he said "two dollars" or "five dollars" if the patient didn't have a nickel—literally, not a nickel?

After all the work Charlie had done just to reach the starting line, now he was racing against some of the toughest conditions in history. Like others surviving the Depression, Charlie became an expert trader. If a man owned a service station, Charlie might treat the man's hernia in exchange for a few free tanks of gasoline, or a discount on a new set of tires. A patient with a chicken coop might pay with surplus eggs. "You got paid in odd ways," Charlie reflected. "I remember one guy, he sold all the insurance on the Plaza, very well-to-do. But the Depression ruined him. I went to see him when he had pneumonia. I took care of him in his home, and when he got over it, he said, 'I don't have a thing to pay you, but would you like a set of *Britannica*s I have?'"

Charlie eyed the volumes of the 1890 edition of the *Encyclopaedia Britannica*, beautifully bound in leather and gracing the man's bookshelf. Charlie needed cash a lot more than he needed reference books. But the books were better than nothing. "I said, 'Well, whatever,' and took the books because that's what this guy had to give me for curing him. And actually, I didn't cure him. Nature cured him of pneumonia."

A scholarly paper published in the depths of the 1930s surveyed thousands of patients in multiple cities and concluded that doctors and other health care providers faced "the problem of giving services free . . . to an extent unknown in any other field. A factory manager was able to economize during hard times by eliminating unproductive departments, by introducing labor-saving devices, or, as a last resort, by closing his plant until the return of prosperity," the authors wrote. "No such expedients were available to the doctor or the hospital director. Business had to continue as usual in spite of the decrease of paying patients and the tremendous increase of free care."

Charlie insisted whenever we talked about those days that he didn't care: he went into medicine as a calling, not to get rich. That didn't make those times any easier, though. He estimated that roughly 40 percent of his calls were never paid for in any form— neither cash nor barter. "You carried them on the books for years, but they weren't paid off," he said of those debts.

Sometimes, after Charlie saw a patient, the family would invite him to share a meal. He told me about another doctor in town who never waited for an invitation. He went straight to the pantry and the icebox whenever he entered a patient's home, and rarely left without eating or taking something.

But medicine could not be practiced entirely on barter. There were fixed expenses. A doctor needed a car. According to that same scholarly paper, medical care in the 1930s came primarily from doctors making house calls. Because they traveled to houses at all hours, ordinary cars would not do. "One thing you had to have as a doctor—something you could not do without—was a spotlight on your car," Charlie said. "Every doctor, soon as he bought a car, had a spotlight put on. The same kind the fire department and police would use. Can you imagine going down a street with no lights, trying to find the house numbers at night?

"I mean, it was impossible," Charlie continued. "You'd spend half your night looking for numbers. We learned every crazy little street in the city. If you ever wanted to know where to find an address, you asked a doctor."

With money so tight, parents were extremely reluctant to alert him when their children were sick. Charlie recalled a time when he was summoned to deal with a boy who had been ailing off and on for the entire winter. His parents had put off calling a doctor, hoping their son would finally get well. Charlie could picture in-flamed tonsils even before he pulled up to the curb.

Entering the unfamiliar home, he sized up the inhabitants, hoping to find a promising assistant. Even the simplest home surgeries were two-person jobs. In a matter of minutes, Charlie could train a brave-looking brother or aunt of the patient to serve as anesthetist, slowly dripping ether onto a wad of cotton in a can attached to a breathing mask. Ether fumes knocked out the patient, and a few drops at regular intervals would keep the patient asleep.

On this call, Charlie found a willing assistant, explained the device, and started the flow of ether. All went well as the patient lost consciousness on the dining room table. Charlie reached into his bag for his wire snare—a loop of sharp wire to surround an infected tonsil. When the loop was pulled tight, the wire sliced the tonsil away.

But in that moment the wire wasn't there.

Charlie dug through his bag. No wire.

His amateur assistant dripped a few drops of ether into the can. He looked at Charlie expectantly. Charlie couldn't imagine halting the procedure now. In desperation, he noticed a picture hanging on the dining room wall. A picture . . .

Picture *wire*.

He pulled the frame from the wall and harvested the wire, pausing to sterilize it over a flame. Then he fed the wire into the snare, looped it around the first tonsil, and drew it tight. A satisfying blossom of blood spread as the offending flesh slipped loose. Charlie repeated the process with the second tonsil. After waiting a bit for the bleeding to stop, he was on his way.

When I heard that story, I pictured Charlie rolling his sleeves down after the surgery, pulling on his jacket, and snapping shut his big leather bag, leaving the house with a bit of a swagger, the tonsils gone, his patient groggy in bed, the picture facedown in its frame on the sideboard awaiting a new wire. It was a memorably resourceful surgery—but far from his most difficult tonsillectomy.

The hardest, he said, were the ones where he arrived to find a house full of children, one of them sick, the others feeling fine. With money tight, the parents would bashfully ask if there might be a discount for taking all the tonsils in the house at once.

In such cases, "the first one was easy," Charlie told me, meaning the first child—the sick one—would agree to climb onto the dining room table. But once the others got a look at what was happening, "they were awfully hard to catch."

Delivering babies was a major source of income, especially after the federal government passed a law at the bottom of the Depression to pay a stipend of twenty-five dollars to doctors for each home delivery. Women and their babies were dying at alarming rates while giving birth without medical assistance. The idea of the stipend was to encourage new mothers to call a doctor, even if there wasn't a nickel in the house. Charlie quickly lost count of the number of babies he delivered. But he never forgot his favorite.

He told me about her once. "Cash was scarce and people couldn't afford to go to the hospital," he said by way of setting the scene. When he arrived at the crowded home, he found a young woman in labor, but something seemed wrong. She did not appear to be at full term.

"I delivered the baby, and it weighed about two pounds," Charlie recalled long afterward. "It was premature. I didn't think it would survive," he continued. "There was nothing like a pediatric intensive care unit in those days, of course. I knew what the hospital would do: they'd put that baby in a warm place and let nature take its course. Well, these people were too poor for the hospital. So I got a shoe box—just an ordinary shoe box—and lined it with cotton and put the baby inside. We put a lamp nearby for warmth, and I fed that baby milk with an eyedropper.

"And do you know? When she was five years old, I took out her tonsils!"

Characteristically, Charlie remembered all of this as an adventure. He recalled the elation he felt when he moved into the grand apartment building. *Dr. White*, with his wife and new career. "I wanted to give a party for a bunch of my friends—the other interns," he said. "One of the doctors that ran the lab at General Hospital gave me a whole gallon of alcohol. Prohibition time, it didn't matter. One hundred percent alcohol! But I didn't have anything to mix it with.

"I knew a patient that owed me twenty dollars, and he hadn't paid me yet. I got on the phone and I called him. I said, 'I'm having a party, and I just got married. I need some money for the mix. Will you pay me?' And he did. He paid me the twenty right away, and I got the mix, and all the guys had mix for their drinks, and we had a party."

It's said that no one in Kansas City was ever convicted of bootlegging during Prohibition. Boss Tom Pendergast ran the city through a mixture of patronage and intimidation. Occasionally, the Boss dipped his toe into good government. Knowing the appetite of voters for decent roads, Pendergast authorized Judge Harry S. Truman to supervise a program of honest infrastructure, putting thousands of unemployed residents to work—and launching Truman's historic career. More typical, though, was Pendergast's arrangement with mob boss Johnny "Brother John" Lazia. A transplant from New York City, Lazia caught the Boss's eye sometime around World War I, when he demonstrated a knack for delivering votes on Election Day from the city's Italian-American residents. The rest of the year, Lazia reliably produced kickbacks from a growing empire of speakeasies and casinos.

As he advanced in power, Lazia kept a little office at police headquarters and was said to have a veto over the hiring or firing of cops. This came in handy when officers were assigned to investigate the frequent shootings in Kansas City's Little Italy—one of which occurred under Charlie's nose during his internship at General Hospital.

"I was making a house call" while serving on ambulance duty, Charlie recalled. "A woman down in Little Italy had pneumonia, and after examining her I decided we needed to take her to the hospital. So I put her on a stretcher, and the driver picked up one end and I took the other. We got her to the door of the house, right next to the street, when here came a big, black sedan with a machine gun, and they gunned down a man right in front of me. And of course they drove on.

"I looked at the ambulance driver and said, 'You know—this guy needs it more than she does.' So we carried her back to bed and loaded the guy who had been shot into the ambulance. I sat in the back as we rushed to the hospital, trying to talk to the guy. But he only spoke Italian. And he didn't speak much, because he died on the way. But my driver was Italian, so I asked him if the guy had said anything about who shot him. He looked at me like I was crazy and said: 'I didn't hear a thing!'"

That was probably wise, because Lazia was a bold gangster. He took pride in his connections with both the upper crust and the underworld. During an epidemic of kidnappings in the 1930s, when even the fashion mogul Nell Donnelly was snatched with her chauffeur from her mansion's driveway, Lazia (it was said) was the man to see to rescue prominent victims. Brother John put the word out, and Donnelly was safely home in a few hours, with zero ransom paid. In Kansas City, Lazia was arguably more powerful than the FBI—for a time. In 1933, when the parking lot at Union Station was the scene of a blazing gunfight between hoodlums and federal agents, Lazia used his police department ties to thwart the investigation.

Charlie wasn't inclined to make trouble, so young Dr. White became popular in Brother John's north-side precincts. He told me about a night when a call summoned him to Little Italy for a woman in labor. When he arrived at the building and walked up to the third-floor apartment, he found the place crowded with nervous relatives, and the patient resting comfortably. Contractions were still far apart. "You had to stay there even though she wasn't ready to deliver. There wasn't any nurse available to check on her," Charlie explained.

As usual, he had sized up the occupants of the home to find the one who seemed most reliable and calm. Now he deputized his chosen assistant to keep an eye on matters while Charlie went downstairs to get some sleep in his car. When the contractions began arriving at a certain interval, he explained, he should be awakened from his nap.

"It was about two o'clock in the morning," Charlie recounted.

The night was warm and the top was down on his Ford Model A convertible. Charlie curled up on the bench seat in back and was quickly fast asleep. But he was startled awake—not by someone saying the baby was coming, but by "two little boys taking the wheels off my car! I guess they didn't see me lying down on the seat, and when I jumped up they were as scared as if they'd seen a ghost. They scattered for sure."

Charlie became well known in the neighborhood. "Medicine was such a personal thing in those days," he used to say. "If you were a family doctor, you went into their homes, you ate their food with them, you knew their people and the way they lived." He came to know the family of one mobster especially well after the man went to jail. "Tax evasion or something," Charlie said with a wave of his hand. The mobster left a sick daughter behind. Charlie took care of the daughter without ever sending a bill while her father was serving his sentence. "He had no money, and I didn't charge him."

Later, when Charlie threw another big party, he remembered his gangster friend with the sick daughter. The mafia man, having served his time, was back on the streets. "I needed some entertainment," Charlie recounted. "I called him. I said, 'Can you find some entertainment for me?' He said, 'Sure'—and sent a truck with a pinball machine and a one-armed bandit."

The party was a smash. Everyone enjoyed the arcade game and the slot machine, and the morning after Charlie called to arrange a pickup. "I said, 'Johnny, we had a great time. Come get your slot machine.' He said, 'Doc, the boys said to let you keep it.'"

The gangster was about to hang up.

"I said, 'Wait, Johnny!'" Charlie did not want to owe a favor to the mob. In that instant, he imagined himself called out some night on a medical errand, only to learn that his "friends" expected him to cover up a murder.

But the slot machine donor didn't budge. "He said, 'Oh, Doc. You just keep that machine.'" Whether Charlie was afraid to insist any further, or whether he accepted the fact that Johnny's gratitude was a virtue all its own—even if the grateful party was not morally spotless—I saw with my own eyes, seventy-five years later, that the slot machine was still in Charlie's basement.

Charlie's stories almost always checked out.

On another call to Little Italy, Mildred decided to ride along and wait in the car while Charlie went upstairs. During his examination, he became vaguely aware of a noise outside. Listening more closely, he realized it was a car horn.

His car horn.

Excusing himself, he rushed outside to find Mildred pressing the horn in fear as two men wrestled and threw fists over the hood of the car. Mildred said she thought he would never come. From Charlie's perspective, he was rescuing Mildred more and more often—and not just from brawling strangers. She battled demons neither of them understood. Married life was a riddle and they lacked the key.

The life of a new doctor's wife in the Depression must have been nothing like the picture in a teenage girl's expectations. Mildred's husband was rarely home. Charlie belonged entirely to his work. He saw patients in his brother-in-law's office every morning and made house calls in the afternoon. He answered calls all night long. And his apartment house listed him as the doctor on standby. Despite all this labor, Charlie wasn't getting ahead. He earned cartons of eggs and tanks of gasoline, surplus slot machines and old encyclopedias.

I picture her loneliness. Mildred had left her parents at the earliest possible moment to live by herself in wide-open Kansas City—what a fiery young woman she must have been. Yet here she was: married, bored, and alone. I've seen the snapshots he kept in an album, showing them fishing and picnicking together. But a photograph was something different in the 1930s. Long before smartphones, and the power to take a thousand pictures without flinching, film was expensive, and each frame counted. No one took pictures of ordinary moments. A photograph was special. So when I saw a snapshot in Charlie's album—a black-and-white document of sun dappling a stream almost a century ago, as the picnic was set out beside the water, and Charlie was relaxed and Mildred was smiling—I began to suspect such moments were rare.

Charlie was stingy with the details of his marriage to Mildred. But as our friendship deepened and we could share moments of pain as well as moments of delight, he let me see briefly how painful those years had been. Sometimes he came home from work to find Mildred in pieces. Sometimes, after a long day, she was gone—and he had no idea where. Two facts that Charlie shared with me suggest how quickly and how terribly things went wrong.

First, Charlie said he decided very early that his wife wasn't stable enough to raise children. They were two young people in their prime baby-making years, yet from that moment Charlie made certain that they would not conceive a child. He didn't share the details with me, but as a doctor, Charlie understood the fertility cycle and knew available contraception methods better than most. His determination could not have made Mildred feel any less isolated or lonely.

The second hard fact was that Mildred went away for several stays at the Menninger family clinic in Topeka, Kansas, about sixty miles west of Kansas City.

At a time when available treatments for mental illness and addiction were backward and sometimes brutal, the Menningers were part of a vanguard. The large farmhouse setting of their clinic was peaceful and bucolic, geared to treatment and healing, not incarceration. Every member of the staff, from janitor to executive, was trained to be part of the therapeutic process. Patients sometimes stayed for months. Karl Menninger, the most public member of the family, shared his expertise with a vast national audience through monthly columns in the popular *Ladies' Home Journal*.

When Mildred came home from her clinic stays, she seemed steadier—but not for long. Nothing had changed at home. Charlie was still working endless hours. Patients were still unable to pay. Mildred was still a mercurial young woman not much beyond childhood herself. If she wanted children, Charlie was too careful, too sensible, too mature to let it happen. Or maybe too wounded by his own father's death to bring a child into so much uncertainty. Coming home, for Mildred, meant returning to boredom and loneliness in Tom Pendergast's booze-soaked city.

Mildred's drinking paused, in other words, but never stopped. Speaking of these years, Charlie admitted that he felt powerless. I think this was, for Charlie, the most difficult admission of all.

His troubles deepened when the Pendergast Machine noticed that a young physician in town—a guy with a mustache that he grew to make himself look older—was an avowed Republican. Charlie

was born in Illinois, Republican country, despite his Rebel fore-
bears. Advised through semi-official channels that it would be
wise to change parties if he wanted to keep his valuable admitting
privileges at General Hospital, Charlie refused. Word came back
that his voting habits might be tolerated if he would—like all city
employees—donate a portion of his income back to the Machine.

Again, Charlie refused.

The hospital kickback scheme was so common that it eventually
became a major scandal. But for Charlie, it was simple. He would not
be bullied, and he paid a big price for his principles. His admitting
privileges were revoked, and he scrambled to latch on with another
institution. He wound up at St. Joseph's Hospital, a red-brick building of three wings in the shape of the letter Y, with ranks of arched
windows marching along the highest floor below a jutting cornice.
Built a few blocks east of Charlie's boyhood home, it was yet another
landmark that he had seen under construction. What Kansas City
called "history," Charlie called "life."

When Adolf Hitler came to power in Germany in 1933, Americans
began to wake up to the threat of another world war. Isolationists
tried to stave it off, insisting that the United States had no national
interests in Europe. Each year eroded that idea a bit further. The
words of Leon Trotsky cast light on the late 1930s. You might not
be interested in war, the Russian revolutionary said prophetically.
But war is interested in you.

For Charlie, war showed its interest in him when "a represen-
tative from the Army came to the hospital and said, 'We'd like to
sign St. Joseph's Hospital as a unit. If we have another war, you guys

will all go together.'" The offer seemed simple enough, and the idea of serving with friends from Kansas City was appealing—if worse came to worst.

It made sense to plan for trouble. This was the Depression, the age of Stalin and Hirohito. "So we joined the regular army" as reserves, Charlie remembered. The team from St. Joseph's did nothing more. There were no meetings or training sessions. Charlie's life went on as before: a doctor struggling to make it in the Depression; a husband trying to save his unhappy marriage. After years of effort, Charlie had plenty of patients, and close to half were paying on time.

Then Japan overran East Asia. Germany rolled into Poland in 1939, conquered France in 1940, and drove Great Britain out of Europe. The St. Joseph's reserve was called to duty.

"Not as a unit, the way they promised," Charlie told me—still resentful many decades later that the offer of a team effort simply evaporated. Charlie was called alone to "a hospital they were building down in the Ozarks. I've forgotten now. It was a big hospital. I jumped in my car and went down there to see fifteen to twenty doctors just sitting around."

The doctors were voicing Charlie's own feelings. There was no hospital waiting for them. The doctors had nothing to do. "They said, 'We're not doing anything. They took us out of our practice, and they haven't even got a hospital yet.'"

Charlie visited the commanding officer and expressed his frustration at being called away for nothing. "Lieutenant," the officer told him, "if you don't like it, resign."

Charlie did.

"I went to St. Louis and resigned from the Army," Charlie

remembered. That lasted a few months, until the war escalated again. "Pearl Harbor came along."

As men and boys from coast to coast rushed to the recruiting offices, Charlie faced a hard decision. At thirty-six, he could stay in Kansas City with his troubled marriage and his growing medical practice. His younger peers would go to war, and he could sweep up their patients. His practice would surely thrive. Or he could serve, and let his patients drift away to doctors who remained behind.

The choice came down to a question of self-esteem. "I thought I was chicken to resign from the Army," he said. So he tried to get back into the nation's service. "I applied to the Navy, and the Navy said, 'Your eyes aren't perfect. We can't take you.' I can't imagine why a doctor needed perfect eyes, but they said no.

"I went over to the Army Air Force, and they took me right away. I actually got a promotion. I resigned as a lieutenant, and they made me a captain when I went back in."

eight

I found it interesting that Charlie worried about being "chicken" when he quit the Army Reserve. Nothing in his life story suggested a lack of physical or psychological courage. Quite the opposite: from his streetcar hopping boyhood to his perilous ride on the front of a locomotive; from his self-advocacy with the Northwestern dean to his experimental transfusion with a dying gangster, again and again Charlie's impulse was to push past whatever natural fears he might have to take action and seize opportunity. Of course, military service involves risk. But service as a doctor—even in wartime—was probably no more dangerous than making emergency calls at night on the streets of Johnny Lazia's Kansas City.

As I learned more and thought more deeply about it, I realized that physical danger was probably not what Charlie was talking about. The big risk in leaving Kansas City to serve his country was the threat posed to Charlie's career, and perhaps to his struggling marriage. It was one thing to leave a salaried job or a wage-earning position to join the military. A soldier's employer might rehire him when the war was over, or another firm might have an open position. This was my grandfather's situation when he left his job as a railroad stationmaster to serve in his second world war. He could trust that his job, or one like it, would still exist when he came home. Charlie had no employer to return to. He lived on the fees he collected from patients, and once those patients went to other doctors, he would be right back where he started, rebuilding from nothing. Nor could he trust that Mildred would be waiting when he came back—though ultimately she was.

So we see that Charlie was risking his life, in a sense, risking the life he had built for himself. Many people today relate to his fear. The killer of careers in the twenty-first century is not a world war; it's the digital revolution, which chews up entire industries and sectors of the economy. My own field, for example: In 2008, what used to be called "newspapers" employed twice as many people in their print and digital newsrooms as they employed in 2020. Half the industry vanished in a dozen years. These massive job losses took their largest toll on people between thirty and fifty years old—the same midlife stage that Charlie had arrived at when he shuttered his practice and entered the Air Force. The story repeats and repeats: department store workers undone by online retailing; stockbrokers replaced by trading platforms; factory workers squeezed out by robots; store cashiers made obsolete by self-scan kiosks. And so on.

It's natural to feel anxiety and even fear amid so much uncertainty. Stoic Charlie, though, understood that every situation is uncertain. Even at our most confident or complacent, we control only our own choices. We never know what lies ahead to challenge, confound, or even cripple us.

Not long ago, I was reminded of the story of Travis Roy, a brilliant young ice hockey player who entered college as one of the most heavily recruited athletes in North America. In 1995 the strapping and handsome freshman earned a spot in the starting lineup at Boston University, defending national champions.

Eleven seconds into his first game with the Terriers, Roy crashed head-down into the boards and broke his spine at the neck. In no more time than it takes to snap your fingers, his life as an elite athlete was over, a possibility he had never imagined. Eleven seconds between a high point of his young life—the first puck drop of what promised to be a sterling college career, followed by years in the pros—and the end of it all.

Eleven seconds.

In a very real sense we are all like Travis Roy, one twist of fate or fickle chance away from some dramatic change. No one can dwell too much on that, but it is good to remember. "Consider how ephemeral . . . all mortal things are," Marcus Aurelius wrote in his *Meditations*. About the same time, in faraway Tibet, the author of a Buddhist scripture wrote the same:

All that is acquired will be lost
What rises will fall
Where there is meeting there will be separation
What is born will surely die

It is the universal wisdom on this precious planet, Earth—the only one we know of where life, and love, and joy are even possible—that nothing is permanent. Whether our ride around the sun is long, like Charlie's, or short, it is but a tremor on the face of time. Rather than be paralyzed by fear of a truth no one can change, surely it's wiser to find and nourish strong selves—identities that we can trust to be worthy no matter what comes next. Deep-down selves. True selves.

Nearly paralyzed from the neck down, Travis Roy found that his gifts went beyond the physical. He was gifted in optimism and determination. When he could no longer express these on the ice, he expressed them in motivational speeches, in raising money for charitable causes, and in the noble way he faced his challenges. His strength and personality drew thousands of people to the meaningful works he championed. After his death in 2020 at age forty-five, I wrote in a newspaper column: "Roy didn't take the ice against North Dakota with the intention of posing existential questions. But 11 seconds later, he put such questions before us. If all the trappings were stripped away, leaving only my true self, who would I be? Am I living fully as that self in every moment? And when it ends, will my story have meaning?"

Over the past half century, scientists have studied the relationship between fear and courage, and what they have found tends to confirm the wisdom of the ancient philosophers. Psychologist S. J. Rachman, in his seminal book *Fear and Courage,* concluded that fear has three components. A feeling of apprehension. A physical response (like a pounding heart, a queasy stomach, a knot of anxiety). And a change in behavior to escape the fear and quiet the response. Courage, Rachman continued, is a deliberate decision to override the change in behavior that is part of fear. The courageous person faces fear, rather than try to escape it.

In other words, without fear, there is no courage. One who senses no danger feels no apprehension. One who feels no apprehension has no desire to run away. Lack of fear, in Rachman's terminology, is not courage. It is simply ignorance of danger.

Stoic philosophers have regarded courage as one of the four most important—cardinal—virtues, along with justice, prudence, and self-control. Lesser virtues serve these four. Courage involves a willingness to choose the right path even when it is difficult or daunting; diligence in pursuing that path; constancy in sticking to the path; fortitude to endure whatever hardships may come along the way.

When Charlie worried about being "chicken," I think he meant that for a moment he lost his Stoic courage. He flinched from his understanding that nothing is certain. But he quickly regained his bearings. Once Charlie thought things through, he realized that staying home from the war would guarantee nothing. Some other twist of fate could just as easily rob him of his medical practice or his marriage—or both. He no more controlled success than a little boy controls whether his father comes home from work alive. But he could do the right thing, which meant volunteering for wartime service. Do it well. And trust that the outcome would be the best that he could make it.

And it was.

Not long before Charlie was born, Orville Wright flew for the first time, covering 102 feet of windswept North Carolina sand dunes in twelve seconds under mechanical power. Charlie was an infant in October 1905, when Orville's brother, Wilbur, made the first true flight, in the sense that he covered a significant distance (more than twenty-four miles), beginning and ending exactly where he chose. The world was changed. Within a dozen years, bombers were sprinkling death over Europe. By the 1930s, aircraft were instruments of indiscriminate violence. Grimly aware that the world was spiraling into another conflagration, and that airplanes would be at the heart of it, U.S. Army engineers began scouring the country for land on which to build airfields and training camps for the legions of pilots, navigators, bombardiers, and mechanics that would be needed to fight a modern war.

One site they chose lay in a parched bottomland between Salt Lake City, Utah, and the Great Salt Lake. Heavy equipment descended on the spot as soon as Japan attacked Pearl Harbor. A city and its airport were built in a matter of weeks. When springtime stirred up its inevitable winds, storms of dust rose so thickly that trucks and jeeps crept over the plain with headlamps blazing at midday. Grit and powder filled bedrolls, mess kits, eyeballs, and ears. Into the dust clouds of Camp Kearns Army Air Field came Captain Charles White.

"They were building a hospital there, and I was one of the first doctors," Charlie recalled. "When you go into service, you tell them all the things you've done. Among all the things I listed, I said I'd given anesthetics.

"So they said, 'You're chief of anesthetics.' They made me head of the laboratory, too. I had to go into town and get technicians to run the lab. That's the Army way. They don't care about experience. We had an awful time in radiology trying to develop specialists. We must have had ten or fifteen different guys go through there. I also had to keep track of the ambulances, see if they were clean and working properly, and I was the personal doctor to the officers. The Army gives you a lot of work."

— 136 —

Twelve months after Pearl Harbor, Camp Kearns was home to some forty thousand trainees and officers, housed in row after row of simple barracks, starkly arrayed on the dead-flat emptiness. Charlie's world revolved around the hospital. It was a big facility—more than one thousand beds—but the cases weren't very interesting. He treated mostly the maladies of fit young men: cuts, burns, and broken bones, heat strokes and mild pneumonias, and lots of infections, many of them sexually transmitted. "It was," he said, "kind of a lark."

The first time Charlie said that to me, I was startled. Later, I thought it one of the most Charlie-like things I'd ever heard. World War II was "kind of a lark." Charlie found joy wherever it might be hiding. At Camp Kearns, a good deal of happiness was to be found in Charlie's gasoline ration book. As personal physician to the camp's officers, Charlie was entitled to as much gasoline as he could burn, despite strict national limits on consumption. He and his friends on the hospital staff "had weekends off." On the other side of Salt Lake City (not a very big place in those days) lay the picturesque Wasatch Mountains, which rise steeply to the east of town. It was less than an hour's drive from camp to the ski trails of Alta. With the base hospital running smoothly by autumn 1942, and snow falling regularly in the mountains, those ski trails beckoned. "They gave me all the gas I wanted," Charlie said with a chuckle. "I'd load my car with guys, and we'd go skiing every weekend."

What matters most about this period for us, though, isn't the fun Charlie managed to find. It is the way he befriended change. World War II was one of history's most powerful engines of change. Innovation came with neck-snapping speed in engineering, manufacturing, logistics, transportation, communication, computing, physical science—and medicine. Two major medical advances directly impacted Captain White and his endangered career, and he made friends with both of them.

The first was the mass production of penicillin, the breakthrough antibiotic medicine. A British scientist, Alexander Fleming, had discovered the strangely powerful compound by accident in 1928. He was growing bacteria in petri dishes in his lab for study purposes. One day he was annoyed to find mold growing on one of the cultures. Looking more closely, he noticed that where the mold was growing, no bacteria survived. What a Stoic moment: Fleming's experiment was apparently ruined, yet because he was doing his best with the thing he could control—his focus, his attention, his brain—he made a vastly greater discovery.

The implications were profound. If doctors could kill harmful bacteria, they might finally be able to cure many of the deadly infections they saw routinely, from blood poisoning to pneumonia to staph. The challenge was to breed the most potent penicillin possible and to prepare it in vast quantities.

Incredibly, this challenge was largely neglected—"one of the disgraces of medical research," in the words of science writer Waldemar Kaempffert—for most of the 1930s, until the outbreak of war. War, the terrible vector of infections, inspired governments in England and the United States to stomp the accelerator on penicillin research, and soon pharmaceutical labs were brewing the miracle mold in enormous vats.

The arrival of antibiotic drugs was an immediate blessing on humanity. Winston Churchill proposed that "Saint Penicillin" should be celebrated with a devotion normally reserved for religion. Yet, at the same time, this advance revolutionized the practice of medicine in ways that spelled the death of Charlie's brand of doctoring. As we've heard him say, Charlie didn't cure disease—no doctors cured diseases before the age of antibiotics. His stock in trade was his "bedside manner," a mixture of knowledge, common sense, kindness, and confidence that comforted and encouraged patients and their families while natural immunity won (or lost) its battle. Without a pill or injection to work a cure, the general practitioner making house calls had to rely on the folks inside the home to carry out instructions after he left. The GP was wellness coach, motivator, and grief counselor rolled into one.

After penicillin, medicine would become a matter of treatments and procedures, more than a matter of care and support. Never again would medical science settle for nature's natural course. Alert to the signs of change, Charlie realized that doctors of the future would not be generalists making house calls with the tools of their trade in a leather bag. They would be specialists who chose a narrow set of treatments or procedures and made a career of delivering cures. Specific expertise would rule in the coming age.

I mentioned two major advances. This is where the second one comes in.

War, with its awful violence, has long been a laboratory for pain management, lifesaving, and surgical techniques. World War II transformed the use of painkillers and anesthesia. Charlie's medical bag in the 1930s held a bottle of ether and a can for inhaling it. As we've seen, a family member of an ailing patient could learn to operate the simple device in minutes. No expertise was needed.

This was the state of the art. Before 1939, there was no certified specialist in anesthesiology in the United States. Money donated to Harvard for a professorship in the field was diverted to more respected work. John S. Lundy of the Mayo Clinic, sometimes called "the father of intravenous anesthesia," recalled that prior to the war, "only those physicians who were incompetent in general practice or in other branches" of medicine were encouraged to specialize in anesthetics. It was a dead end for medical careers.

War produced an arsenal of painkilling and pain-blocking techniques. Advances in trauma surgery accelerated the use of endotracheal tubes to open airways, support breathing, and administer anesthetics. Doctors perfected the use of sodium thiopental and other numbing drugs administered through IV lines. They realized the value of local and regional blockers that could shut off pain in one part of the body without putting a patient entirely under.

These head-spinning changes came so quickly that one of Lundy's colleagues, Ralph Tovell, was commissioned by the War Department to survey the need for anesthetic specialists. His October 1942 report—delivered as Charlie was discovering the ski slopes of Alta—urgently recommended more training in anesthesiology for military doctors of all kinds. Tovell pitched in personally, delivering a two-hour lecture on anesthetic techniques to hospital staffs throughout the European Theater. Stateside, the National Research Council convened a panel of experts, including Lundy of the Mayo Clinic, to create a crash course for anesthesiologists.

Charlie reached out and seized his future.

Having mentioned his experience with ether during his Air Force induction, Charlie was the designated expert in anesthetics at Camp Kearns. Now, with so much urgent attention on anesthesiology, he was promoted and given a new assignment. Major White was to report to Lincoln Army Air Field in Lincoln, Nebraska. The facility collected trainees from bases across the country and formed them into units before sending them into combat. "The pilots, co-pilots, bombardiers—all of them gathered at Lincoln," Charlie explained. His assignment was to be chief of anesthesiology at the new base hospital.

"I was going to be the big-shot chief," Charlie explained. "But I said, 'Look. I'm just not geared up for that. You're going to have to train me.' I couldn't say no, I won't go. But I could say, 'You had better train me.'"

That's how Charlie found himself in 1943 in Rochester, Minnesota, at the Mayo Clinic, in the department of John S. Lundy. Lundy's research council team had designed a three-month immersion course, heavy on practical experience, to turn general practitioners into anesthesiologists. Charlie was among the first "ninety-day wonders" to receive the training. He breezed through the course, fascinated and excited by the advances he was learning. Then he traveled to Lincoln to finish out the war.

Just like that, Charlie had turned the threat of change into an opportunity to grow. No longer was he an endangered general practice doctor trying to hang on to a precarious piece of a dying field. Instead, when the war ended, he would return home as a pioneer in a new and rapidly growing specialty—one of the first anesthesiologists in Kansas City, and with a Mayo Clinic seal of approval to boot.

To me, this episode contains the essence of Charlie's life. Realism and optimism fit together powerfully. Too many people believe that realism—seeing the world as it is, with all its pain and threats—demands a pessimistic response. The optimist is deluded, they believe, a Pollyanna moving blindly through a bleak existence with a dumb smile. Charlie was realistic about the dead end he had reached as a bag-carrying doctor making house calls. Penicillin and its successor drugs had changed the doctor's role. Yet, at the same time, he was optimistic about new beginnings, and confident in his ability to grab them. Charlie was alert to the next open door, and when he saw it, he strode through.

Many people, in times of uncertainty (and all times are uncertain), want the answers all at once. How will today's trends shape tomorrow's world? What will life look like in the future? Charlie understood that we don't live in the world's future; we live in our own present moment, inside the much smaller zone of our own actions and our own will. We can't control tomorrow: that's realism. But optimism teaches that we can watch for tomorrow, seek to understand it, and leap when the moment arrives to grasp it—perhaps even to shape it.

Charlie entered the U.S. Army Air Forces in 1941 with a measure of dread about what it would do to his career. He left the service in 1946 eager for the next phase. "After the atomic bombs, there wasn't much need for new flight crews, so we were all just sitting around bored," he remembered. The wait for discharge papers felt interminable. Typically, Charlie did what he could.

"I wrote a big letter," he recounted. In it, Charlie listed reasons why he could do far more good at home than cooling his heels in Lincoln. His fellow officers were suspicious when his discharge was approved "within two weeks." Charlie must have pulled strings with the new president of the United States, who hailed from Kansas City, his envious colleagues noted. "They said, 'You know Truman, and you called Truman.'"

Which showed what they knew of Kansas City. In fact, Charlie was pushed out of Kansas City General Hospital by Truman's friend and patron Tom Pendergast. "No, guys, I just sent a letter," Charlie insisted. "A letter through regular channels."

Nevertheless, Charlie went home with a head start.

He wore his Army greens, with insignia reflecting his last promotion to lieutenant colonel, and went straight to St. Joseph's Hospital. There, he told me, "my friends put me right to work giving anesthetics." His midcareer shift from general practice to a specialty had worked perfectly. Instead of coming home to a dead end, he found a new route forward.

I wish I had thought to ask Charlie about a character missing from the story of his return: Mildred. I can only guess that she wasn't waiting patiently for him, because the house he had rented after their Villa Serena years was occupied by subletters, and in the desperate postwar housing shortage the tenants refused to move out. Charlie found a room at the Hyde Park Hotel and began scouring the city for rental housing. When, after months of searching, he finally found an available place, he persuaded his tenants to take it. He had his home back at last.

Mildred returned sometime afterward, because she reappeared in the stories he told of his rapid rise in Kansas City's medical community. With his new specialty and his wartime managerial experience, Charlie became a driving force in the introduction of anesthesiology to Missouri and Kansas. His practice boomed as the city's leading surgeons sought him out for their teams. In his spare time, Charlie organized a professional association for the quickly growing number of doctors following him into the field. When she was able, Mildred pitched in to arrange activities for the wives of anesthesiologists while their husbands were meeting. (In those days, there were few woman doctors.)

But there were many times when Mildred wasn't able. Once he understood that I had experience with loved ones who suffered from mental illness and substance abuse, Charlie was open with me about his pain over Mildred's suffering—and his own. He told me of his repeated efforts to find help for his wife at the rehabilitation facilities then known as "sanitariums," including the Menninger Clinic. The stays became more frequent and of longer duration. "She was up and down, up and down," said Charlie. "She'd say she had 'the jitters.'"

Her official diagnosis was hypoglycemia, insufficient sugar in the blood, which can lead to depression, irritability, memory loss, anxiety, and disorientation. But the low blood sugar was a symptom of something else: alcoholism, possibly compounded by an eating disorder and aggravated by barbiturate pills.

Mildred was home in early 1948. Charlie recalled taking her on vacation to Cuba—"had a ball down there"—and returning by early April for a meeting of the regional chapter of the American Society of Anesthesiologists. Charlie was the local secretary that year. Mildred was welcoming the wives. The meeting ended on April 6 with cocktails and dinner at the swanky Hotel President in downtown Kansas City.

The day had been busy. Doctors in attendance learned about the value of airway tubes for chest surgery. At last it was possible to open the chest without collapsing the lungs—a technique developed during the war that was now spreading across the country and saving lives. The dinner speaker admonished the audience that the old ways of doing medicine no longer applied.

Midway through the meal, Mildred whispered to Charlie that she wasn't feeling well. He could stay, but she needed to go home. She left—but she didn't go home. When Charlie arrived at their house a few hours later, his wife had vanished.

Mildred's body was discovered the next day at the Gladstone Hotel, about a mile from the President and a long way down in prestige. Charlie told me she committed suicide by swallowing a fatal dose of sleeping pills. I have the police report, thanks to my wife's skillful digging. Karen knew a report had to exist in some musty file, and as a former White House reporter, she refused to quit until she found it.

Officer Elmer Murphy of the Kansas City Police Department answered a call at 3:05 p.m., April 7, 1948. The hotel maid, Beatrice Gaines, told Officer Murphy that she opened the door to Room 405 at 8:30 a.m. to clean the room—but quickly closed it again after glimpsing a naked woman on the bed. Gaines returned near the end of her shift, just before checkout time, 3 p.m. The figure on the bed had not moved. The maid told her boss, and police were called.

Next, Officer Murphy interviewed a front desk clerk, Steven Drew, who said the woman on the bed checked in the previous night at 7 p.m. in the company of a man. The pair carried no luggage. They registered as Mr. and Mrs. Charles W. Koehler of Independence, Missouri. The clerk described "Koehler" as forty-two years old, a little less than six feet tall, around 175 pounds, with a "dark complexion and . . . a foreign look about him." Drew noticed the man's stylish brown suit.

Drew's shift had ended at 11 p.m. the previous night and he did not return to work until 2 p.m.—an hour before the maid sent up the alarm. So he never saw "Koehler" leave.

Detective Keiffer Burris of the homicide squad was summoned. He arrived along with a doctor from General Hospital, who examined Mildred's body and found no sign of injury. Her death was ascribed to "natural causes." The next day's newspaper elaborated, slightly: "Death was the result of hypoglycemia and complications." If the room contained any signs of drugs or alcohol, the police were too polite to mention it in their report.

The body in the hotel room was quickly matched to the missing persons report Charlie had filed earlier that morning. I don't know whether police called him to the hotel or whether he identified Mildred at the morgue later. Investigators turned over two rings— an engagement ring and a wedding ring that Mildred was wearing when she died—and the gold Bulova watch she had on her wrist.

Detective Burris promised in his report to "endeavor to locate Charles Koehler," but I don't think he looked very hard. No record of a search can be found, and I doubt Charlie had much interest in tracking the man down. Suppose "Koehler" was found, and suppose he explained how it happened that the wife of Dr. Charles White left a meeting where her husband was enjoying his new prominence and met a dark, well-dressed gentleman who took her immediately to a hot-sheet hotel. Such testimony could only serve to embarrass Charlie and further stigmatize his wife. Instead a blanket of silence settled over Mildred's sad life and depressing death.

Charlie's helplessness in the face of his wife's disease was still raw more than six decades later when he told me the story. Could he have done more to help her? I have no way to judge. I do know that treatment at the Menninger Clinic was about as good as anyone could find in those days. Clinic doctors were early adopters of the idea that addiction is a disease, not a moral failure. But this was also a time when some so-called experts still believed that women could not be addicts, certainly not a respectable doctor's wife.

Nor was there a network of support for Mildred when she returned home from treatment. Alcoholics Anonymous had only recently arrived in Kansas City. Its original "clubhouse," on the Kansas side of town, was not convenient to the couple's home, nor would Mildred have been likely to meet another woman if somehow she had heard about the program. Very few women nationwide participated in twelve-step sobriety in the 1940s. The first residential facility to offer a twelve-step program—Hazelden, a clinic near Minneapolis—did not open until 1949. Too late for a troubled young doctor's wife in a city known far and wide for its booze.

Charlie married again after a few years. He wasn't ready, as it turned out. And yet, the more I learned about his second marriage—thanks, again, to my wife's ability to find things that other people believe to be lost forever—the more I wished the marriage had worked out.

Or maybe not. Life is a sequence of hits and misses, of near misses and false starts and their consequences. If Charlie's second marriage had succeeded, he might never have owned the house across the street from mine. I wouldn't have admired his jaunty golf club cane. I would never have seen him washing his girlfriend's car, nor learned any part of his story.

Life unfolds by accident, despite our hopes and plans. We can't unwish the accidents without wishing away our lives. So let me say just this: Charlie and his second wife could have made a dazzling pair.

When Charlie White "ran across" Jean Landis, as he once put it, they were two good-looking people with a lot of spunk, two lovers of life, two takers of risks. Theirs was a rapid romance, as was often the case after the war. People were eager to make up for lost time. When Charlie married Jean in her parents' living room, he must have thought it was going to work.

It didn't work.

Jean Landis was born in 1918 in California, roughly a dozen years younger than Charlie. As a girl, she wanted to fly, inspired by the likes of Amelia Earhart, one of America's Depression-era heroines. With World War II, Jean's chance arrived. Young men were being blown from the sky by the thousands, until there were not enough male pilots to wage the war with airmen left over to move planes around the country. Necessity created the WASPs: the Women Airforce Service Pilots program. A civilian organization, it offered no rank or glory. But the program allowed young women the opportunity to fly cutting-edge warplanes—and more than that, a chance to serve.

WASP pilots mastered every aircraft in the American arsenal. They met fighters, bombers, and transports as the planes rolled off assembly lines, then flew the birds to the coasts, where they were shipped to war zones. About 1,000 women served as WASPs. Together they flew 60 million miles. They earned $150 per month. Thirty-eight of them died on duty.

I've seen a photograph of Jean taken around 1944. She wears a flight suit that nicely complements her willowy figure, goggles, and lipstick as she stands on the wing of a P-51 Mustang, her favorite plane. The Mustang was the warplane that gave the Allies unquestioned command of the skies, because the powerful fighter-bomber had enough range to protect bomber fleets all the way from base to target and back. Jean flew Mustangs carefully and soberly when she was in sight of the runway. But when she was alone over the American prairie, she put each plane through its paces. A farmer on his tractor, or children playing in a field, might look up to see, in an otherwise empty blue sky, a buzzing little dart turning a sudden barrel roll. That could have been Jean.

Nearing an airfield one day, she radioed for permission to land. About the same time, another pilot, a man, reported seeing a Mustang headed for the airstrip. The controller toggled his radio for information from the incoming superplane.

Jean asked again for permission to land.

Get out of the way! the flight controller shouted at Jean. *There's a P-51 coming in.*

"I *am* the P-51!" Jean answered, and dropped her plane onto the tarmac.

When the end of the war was in sight, Jean took her last official flight. Above New York Harbor, she turned on impulse to circle the Statue of Liberty with tears in her eyes. Then she flew on to her final landing as a WASP.

More than sixty years later, in 2009, Congress gave its highest honor, the Congressional Gold Medal, to Jean Landis and her WASP comrades. By then, thanks to her charisma, Landis was among the most celebrated of the surviving woman flyers. But her service was unheralded when Jean hung up her goggles and returned to her civilian life. She went to college, earned a degree in physical education, and landed a job as a teacher at what was then Park College, on the banks of the Missouri River. From the center of campus at the top of a bluff, the Kansas City skyline was visible to the east.

She soon met a widower with a mustache and a sense of adventure. She was young and eager. He was wounded and wary. They jumped. And almost as soon as they married, she discovered her mistake. "He was a little too possessive," she said of Charlie many years later.

But by the time I heard this, Charlie had told me his version of the story more than once. Indeed, he must have told it many times to me and others, because he had boiled what must have been a terrible disappointment down to a few insouciant sentences. He said his second wife drove away in his convertible with his golf clubs and the silverware in the back. "She was a great gal," he said airily, but what could a guy expect from a "woman PE teacher." "She didn't want to be married," Charlie seemingly concluded, only to add, "Her acquaintances were all female."

Left by a lesbian who realized her mistake? My wife demanded more explanation. She squeezed the internet after Charlie's death until the story of Jean Landis, WASP heroine, popped out. In passing, a writer had quoted her saying that she was briefly married to a midwestern doctor.

She squeezed harder and discovered that Jean was still alive.

Squeezed harder, and found a telephone number.

The former Mrs. Charles White was nearing her own one hundredth birthday when Karen jangled her phone. Jean Landis was sparkly and sharp and happy to tell the story. She agreed that she came to a realization after marrying Charlie—but her insight had to do with Charlie, not with herself. Landis said she married Charlie without realizing how much damage he had suffered while living with Mildred. She thought she had found a kindred spirit, and she liked him. "He was such a gentleman, thoughtful, fun, very levelheaded."

But Charlie, in his grief, forgot everything that he knew about living. Having suffered with Mildred, he appeared determined not to get hurt again. Landis said that Charlie couldn't stand to have an hour go by without knowing where she was and what she was doing. "It's like he didn't trust me," she said on the phone.

She continued generously: "It was probably my fault. I'm a very independent, smart woman. He hoped I would be the kind of wife who would hang out with the other wives sipping cocktails at the clubhouse, but that wasn't my style. I felt that he was on my back."

Jean said there was no convertible and no golf clubs. When she decided to end the marriage, she drove her own Buick. She called Charlie to let him know that she was going, and he offered to send her some money, but Jean didn't need any help.

"You don't owe me anything," she said with tenderness.

Charlie was alone.

nine

There is a wonderful image in *Les Misérables*—Victor Hugo's sprawling novel, not the wildly successful musical lightly based on it. Hugo compares the soul of a thriving individual to the workings of the human eye, which adjusts to gloom by becoming more open. "The pupil dilates in darkness and in the end finds light," the author observes, "just as the soul dilates in misfortune and in the end finds God."

I never heard Charlie talk much about God. The nearest he came with me was to say lightheartedly that he went to church in old age because he was "cramming for the final." But this idea of expanding the soul, of opening wider to the world, in response to misfortune captures something important about Charlie's approach to pain. If anything, after Mildred's tragic death and the failure of his marriage to Jean Landis, Charlie lived larger—not in the sense of extravagance, but in the way he seized experience and pressed the juice from it. He doubled down on his naturally affirmative nature, his inclination to say yes: yes to adventure, yes to experiment, yes to new ideas. Charlie lived in full, not in part, and thereby connected to a life force, a spring of hope, that some might want to call God.

Worlds opened to Charlie, quite literally. There was a day in the early 1950s when a doctor named Wally Graham reached out to him. Graham needed Charlie's help with a delicate matter of international diplomacy. Could he drop everything for an emergency trip to Peru?

Let me back up to paint the picture.

Charlie was extremely busy as one of the city's trailblazing anesthesiologists, often participating in twenty or more surgeries per day. His reputation grew until he was the go-to favorite of many of the best doctors in town. Perhaps the most famous was General Wallace Harry Graham, the official White House physician. Graham was a second-generation Kansas City doctor. His father, a general practitioner from the days before antibiotics, was a friend of Harry S. Truman. The elder Dr. Graham had served with Truman in the Army Reserve, where Truman aspired to a spot on the doctor's pistol-shooting team. However, Truman's eyesight was so bad he could barely see the targets.

Friendships meant a lot to Truman, who kept up on Graham's family even as he went to Washington to join the U.S. Senate in 1935. Ten years later, Truman was sworn in as vice president. The politician knew that old Dr. Graham's son Wally had followed his father into medicine, won a fellowship to study in Europe, and was serving with distinction in the European war.

When Franklin D. Roosevelt died on April 12, 1945, Truman was thrust into the presidency. By the time of his summit meeting with Stalin and Churchill three months later, the new president was still assembling his own staff. Heading to the German city of Potsdam, near Berlin, Truman thought about his friend's talented son as his White House doctor. Wally Graham was already in Europe, already in uniform, and already a known commodity. Summoned to Potsdam, Wally Graham protested that he was a surgeon, not an internist. Truman waved dismissively. "I know all about you," Truman said, "and I've known you from cradle up to the present time."

Wally Graham had an easy smile and a gift of gab, and Truman soon realized he could be a useful diplomatic tool. Truman insisted that Lord Halifax, the British ambassador, bring his twinges and troubles to Graham's office at the White House. When King Ibn Saud, founder of Saudi Arabia, found his arthritis unbearable, Truman dispatched Graham along with a pain management team to see the king in Riyadh.

Now Manuel Odría, president of Peru, needed surgery to repair a clawlike hand. Graham wanted Charlie to accompany him to Lima to handle the anesthesia.

Fairly or not, Charlie had his doubts about Wally Graham's surgical proficiency. These doubts might have been personal: Graham could be pretty strong coffee. He loved to brag about meeting Sigmund Freud, and capturing Hitler's last will and testament, and the many times he was wounded in battle (though somehow he never got the medals he was entitled to). Graham was a major general and the president's personal physician before the age of forty—and he acted the part. It's also possible that Charlie's low opinion was influenced by politics: Graham raised the ire of the American Medical Association, and of Republican doctors like Charlie, by promoting Truman's plan for national health insurance.

Whatever the explanation, Charlie told me that he worried the surgery might prove complex and that Graham could create an international incident by crippling the Peruvian president. He asked why the surgery couldn't be done in the States. Graham replied that Odría was concerned about being deposed in a coup if he left the country. So Charlie said he would go on one condition: that the mission also include a specialist named Bill Duncan, one of Charlie's closest friends.

It turned out that no great delicacy was required. Odría was suffering from an annoying but not life-threatening condition, Dupuytren's contracture, in which fibrous tissue causes fingers to curl inward. According to Graham's unpublished memoirs, Charlie numbed the presidential paw with Novocain and Graham cut the fibers loose—for which he was awarded a life membership in the Peruvian Surgical Society. I think it's more likely that Charlie instead used the new and superior local anesthetic lidocaine.

However he was numbed, Odría was delighted with the results. As a sign of his gratitude, he instructed the Peruvian navy to take the visiting doctors on a journey into the Amazon rain forest. For Charlie, this was when the trip became magical. He couldn't care less about membership in the Peruvian Surgical Society; experience, rather than honors, mattered most to him.

"So then we flew over the Andes," Charlie recalled, to the remote rubber capital of Iquitos. There Peruvian sailors met the doctors for a trip few Americans had ever made. "A navy boat took us down the river. Wally acquired a shotgun someplace. Bill Duncan and I had machetes. We'd leave the boat and play like we were explorers— Wally with his gun and Bill and I with machetes. We ran across about a twelve-foot python and Wally shot it."

At a remote village in the vast rain forest, they met a man selling monkeys. Charlie bought one and named him "Bill Duncan." Duncan bought one and named his "Charlie White." They kept the monkeys in "a little basket" until they reached Panama on their way home. Now they faced the problem of importing wildlife to the United States.

As Charlie told the story, the diplomatic doctors discovered that they were in the same Panama City hotel with the crew that would be serving on their homeward-bound aircraft. They asked the flight attendants to dinner, had a swell time, and enlisted them in a plan to smuggle the monkeys aboard. (Of Charlie and Bill, an airline hostess once said: "I've never seen two better-looking men.") "They helped us get these monkeys home. We just carried them on the plane," Charlie recounted.

Duncan had a wife and family in Kansas City, so his monkey didn't last long. But bachelor Charlie kept his for years. "It grew to about two feet tall. I had to build a cage down in the basement." Charlie dreamed big for his monkey, and tried to train the animal to ride his prize Irish setter like a horse. But the monkey was having none of it. "I never could tame him," Charlie said wistfully. Still, there were laughs. Charlie took his monkey out for drives in his convertible, and when he passed a fruit stand, he shouted: "Would you give my boy here a banana?" Though wild, the monkey grew fond of Charlie, almost possessive, and sprayed urine from his cage whenever Charlie introduced a new girlfriend.

Another trip began with an invitation from a pilot friend. Trans World Airlines wanted the pilot to pick up a plane under repair in Africa and bring it back to corporate headquarters, which was then in Kansas City. How would Charlie like to tag along as navigator?

"I don't know how!" Charlie scoffed, but his friend assured him it would take no great skill to double-check the compass heading.

Never one to pass up an adventure, Charlie cleared his schedule and found a medical conference in Switzerland that he would duck into, thus making the trip tax-deductible. From there he hopped into Egypt, before heading to South Africa to meet his friend. "But the plane wasn't ready," Charlie recounted, "so I took a trip through Kruger National Park." His two-day safari by automobile carried him through some of the finest wildlife habitat on the continent. Charlie "saw elephants and lions and hippos in the river." Exotic animals would come right up to the vehicle, he remembered, and peer in at Charlie as if he were a creature in a zoo. Charlie was delighted. But back in Johannesburg, the airplane still wasn't ready, so Charlie's pal introduced him to another TWA pilot headed back to Europe.

This new friend proved quite obliging. When Charlie expressed a hope that he might glimpse Victoria Falls, the pilot made room for Charlie in the copilot's seat and flew so close that the mist from the falls clouded the plane windows. "I don't know what the other passengers must have thought," Charlie mused. Traveling on an open ticket, he stopped for a few days in Malta, where French police were enforcing a curfew, then paid a visit to Spain, ducked into the Netherlands, and finally pointed for home.

He was just as adventuresome in familiar surroundings. Part of Charlie's adaptability to a century of great changes was the delight he found in things new and untried. He wasn't self-conscious about the risk of failure. That's how he found himself in a pasture one day, wearing his mask and gown, using a fireplace bellows as a respirator for a horse.

I'll let Charlie explain. "We had a doctor friend who raised race-horses. One of his best animals, named Hickory Chuck, tore some ligaments in his leg. The standard veterinary treatment in those days was to take a hot iron and try to fuse the ligaments together, but that just didn't work.

"Well, there was an orthopedic specialist at St. Joseph's Hospital named Garrett Pipkin, and when he heard about this he said he thought he could devise a procedure to sort of fold those ligaments and sew them together. They wanted me to immobilize the horse.

"But there's a problem, right? If I put the horse out completely, he'll fall over and might injure himself worse. I decided to use a little bit of a paralyzing agent, Anectine, we call it. We devised this big board and strapped the horse to it so the animal would remain standing. I gave him the Anectine—it didn't take much of a dose to completely paralyze the horse—and then I put the bellows from my fireplace in the horse's nose and pumped in air to keep him breathing."

Pipkin made quick work of the surgery and soon Charlie was bringing the horse out of paralysis. The repair was successful. Hickory Chuck resumed his racing career. Charlie's only regret was that the experiment was not filmed. "I wish we had a movie," he said. "There we were, in white operating gowns and masks and gloves out in the pasture with a horse strapped to a board. I can't imagine what people made of all that if they saw us."

One of the riskiest frontiers of medicine in the 1950s—and therefore most exciting to Charlie—was open-heart surgery. Like penicillin and anesthesia, cardiac surgery got a boost from World War II. A young

American doctor billeted to a London military hospital, Iowa-born Dwight Harken, despaired over the soldiers who arrived with shards of shrapnel in their hearts. Conventional wisdom held that the heart was inviolate; therefore, there was no way to extract these metal fragments. A heart wound was a death sentence.

Harken reasoned that if the soldiers were going to die anyway, there was no harm in trying to save them. He experimented with finger-size incisions in the heart wall to allow him to reach quickly inside and remove the shrapnel. The gamble was a huge success: Harken saved more than 125 lives without losing a single patient.

After the war, Harken and others realized that the same technique might be useful in treating a condition known as mitral valve stenosis, a potentially fatal condition that often resulted when a youthful strep throat infection worsened into rheumatic fever. Fibrous tissue inside the heart caused the mitral valve to narrow, leading to high blood pressure, blood clots, blood in the lungs, and even heart failure.

Charlie and his colleagues in Kansas City were intrigued to read in medical journals about experimental surgery to repair stenotic valves. "The surgeon could reach in real quick and make a little incision in the heart. And with his finger, he probed the valve to find that fibrous tissue, and stretch the valve, break the adhesion, and get out," Charlie recalled. "Start to finish, the whole thing could be done in under an hour."

There was a catch, however. The idea of a heart-lung machine that could control a patient's circulation during surgery was still on the drawing board. Even a relatively brief valve surgery ran a high risk of death unless the flow of blood through the heart could be slowed dramatically.

Researching the matter further, Charlie learned of experiments in which patients under anesthesia were chilled to reduce their body temperature. "When their temperature dropped from the high nineties, which is normal, into the eighties, well, the blood gets sort of thick and so you don't bleed so much," Charlie explained.

Thus, to pioneer open-heart surgery in Kansas City, Charlie simply needed to figure out how to safely chill an unconscious patient. He was pondering this challenge one day after work, as he tended a few horses he had purchased with a little land south of town. It was a sign of his thriving new career as a specialist that he was now able to indulge his lifelong passion for raising and riding horses just as his grandfather, the cavalryman, had done.

As Charlie worked, his eye fell on the large oval trough—known as a horse tank—that held water for his livestock. In a flash, he realized this was just what he needed. A horse tank was large enough to hold a sleeping patient buried in ice. Charlie reported to his surgical team that he had the answer they sought.

"So I bought a horse tank and we put the patient under anesthesia and packed him in ice," Charlie told me. "We brought his temperature down to about eighty-six degrees Fahrenheit—not cold enough to kill him but cold enough that the blood slows way down. We lifted him from the tank full of ice, placed him on the operating table, and quickly the surgeon opened the chest and made an incision in the heart. He went inside, broke up the fibrous tissue, sewed him back up, and it was done. In an hour, the patient was all thawed out."

Charlie's horse tank served as the leading edge of cardiac surgery in Kansas City for some time, and "we never lost a patient." When the heart-lung machine was developed, icing patients became a relic of the medical dark ages, only a step or two more advanced than leeches. Surgeons now could spend hours inside the heart, not just stretching valves but replacing them, reopening arteries and veins—even transplanting healthy hearts in place of diseased ones. But before such things were routine, heart surgery was an audacious miracle, and a horse tank full of ice was wizardry.

This story says a lot about Charlie's talent for navigating change. He had lived less than half of his life span, and already his formal education had been rendered largely obsolete. As rudimentary as horse-tank heart surgery now appears, it was inconceivable when Charlie was in medical school a generation earlier. Then, doctors lacked the antibiotics to make open-heart surgery safe. They had no understanding of heart tissue as a muscle that could be operated on. They lacked anesthetics and airway management skills to make multistep surgery possible.

Charlie had a natural feeling for the approach to change that later came to define Silicon Valley. Known as IID—iterative and incremental development—this philosophy recognized that great transformations rarely come as single thunderbolts. Maybe Isaac Newton really did understand gravity when an apple dropped on his noggin, but in most cases discovery and change come one step at a time. Thomas Edison tested six thousand filaments to find the best one for his lightbulb.

Iterative and incremental development is a supremely practical, pragmatic, approach to change—professional change as well as personal change. Don't insist on a perfect solution before tackling a problem. Move step by step (that's the incremental part), improving with each new learning experience (that's the iterative part).

Charlie embraced the fact that he would be learning new things as long as he lived. His education at school was the beginning, not the end—not by a long shot. He moved forward by accepting that he would advance in small increments, not just giant leaps. Open-heart surgery wouldn't arrive in fully formed glory, like a Hollywood ending. It would creep forward a bit at a time. Progress might spend a year or two in an ice bath rigged from farm equipment. But things would be learned at each step to make the next steps possible.

This is how we live with change. This is how even elderly and change-resistant people learn to pump their gasoline with a credit card reader and watch their great-grandchildren take first steps on social media. More important, this is how innovation races ahead. Change doesn't wait for an apple to fall on someone's head. Thousands or millions of Charlie Whites take little steps into the future. They see how a horse tank might be a step forward.

They give it a try.

For people trying to thrive in uncertainty, iterative and incremental development is a consolation. It says, don't try to solve everything. Stop demanding answers to every question about your life and career. Look instead for a small step forward.

Just answer the next question. Find the next step. And take it.

Charlie was also willing to make mistakes. He told me he was glad to have worked in an era before malpractice lawsuits were common. "We could be innovative and not fear the stab of the lawyers, you know?" Charlie once explained. "I took part in something like forty thousand surgeries, and I never was sued. I made mistakes. Sometimes I would intubate someone with bad teeth and, well, you barely touch them and they break off. I would go by the bed after they woke up, give them twenty-five dollars, and say, 'Go get that tooth fixed.' That was it."

After the war, when a buddy suggested that Charlie should invest in a fledgling Colorado ski resort called Aspen, he scoffed: "That's just a ghost town!" Definitely a mistake. At one point he owned sixty acres of lakefront property a half hour east of Kansas City. He kept horses there and enjoyed hosting the nuns from St. Joseph's Hospital for riding excursions—made slightly comical by the habits they wore. But he sold the land for far less than it would be worth when the city's elite lined the lakefront with multimillion-dollar mansions.

Another mistake.

His timing was no better with the little farm south of town, which he sold—then watched as it was subdivided into some of the city's most desirable real estate. I once commented on the various fortunes he had missed, and he cheerfully replied that I didn't know the half of it. A salesman by the name of Ewing Kauffman once tried to interest Charlie in a start-up business he had launched in his basement. "He was cleaning oyster shells in a washing machine and grinding them into antacid powder," Charlie said, still slightly incredulous. Charlie held on to his money. Kauffman's business, called Marion Labs, was ultimately a major pharmaceutical company worth billions.

Another mistake.

Yet Charlie seemed to derive as much delight from recalling these blunders as he did from remembering his triumphs. He had an understanding that mistakes can have virtue. They show that we are making the effort, engaging with life, "in the arena," as Theodore Roosevelt famously put it. Another president, Harry Truman, said: "Imperfect action is better than perfect inaction." There is value in making decisions, right or wrong, and moving on. Perfectionism, by contrast, can become an enemy of life itself, freezing us in place while the world goes on without us.

There is no living without making mistakes. As Epictetus, that marvelous Stoic, said, "If you want to improve, be content to be thought foolish and stupid." The Nobel Prize–winning physicist Niels Bohr had a slightly different spin on the same truth. "An expert," he declared, "is a person who has made all the mistakes that can be made in a very narrow field." Or think of it this way: a warrior is known not just by muscle and valor, but by scars.

Charlie was now on the weather side of fifty, and though he was single and had no children, he was very much a family man. He was devoted to his mother, who had been named Missouri Mother of the Year by the missionary society where she worked. And he was close to his sisters, one of whom kept his office running, scheduling surgeries and balancing the books. Her duties included running Charlie's household. This didn't strike everyone in Charlie's social circle as the best arrangement, and his partner's wife suggested a better one. "She decided I ought to have a wife," he recounted.

Presented with this conclusion, Charlie demurred. His experiences with marriage had not been easy. He wasn't interested in trying again. But the partner's wife was one step ahead of him. That's perfect, she dissembled. There's a widow who lives on my block, Lois Grimshaw, and she doesn't want to get married again, either. Be a dear and invite her to the big poker party I am planning.

So Charlie was a dear and agreed to escort the widow to the poker party. When he knocked on her door, an assertive eight-year-old answered. This was Julie.

Are you here to date my mother? she demanded.

Yes, I am, Charlie replied.

Are you a doctor? the girl continued. "Because you smell like one."

Thus welcomed, Charlie entered the house, trying discreetly to sniff himself for the odor of the operating room.

Then he saw Lois.

She was breathtaking. As a Dallas teenager, she had appeared as a model in advertisements for the Neiman-Marcus department store. The local newspaper pronounced her hands the loveliest in the city. She had dark hair and fair skin and elegant features. Her eventual son-in-law Jack Moore summed her up this way: "I really, really loved Lois. She was a beautiful woman—and she knew how to handle men."

Intrigued, Charlie walked her down the street to his partner's house, where Lois took a seat at the poker table and played like she was raised in a casino. By the end of the night, as Charlie looked at her across the table behind her mountain of chips, he was smitten. "She was beautiful and a great card player," he said with a shrug half a century later.

Charlie became the father of a son and two daughters when they married. They had two more girls together. His relationship with Lois's teenage son Bill was distant. Charlie seemed almost disinterested when Bill served gallantly in Vietnam and then built a career in the law. That's how it seemed to Bill, anyway. And I have to admit that (for whatever this is worth) Charlie rarely spoke of his stepson to me. They shared something tragic and intense: the loneliness of only sons who have prematurely lost their fathers. Sadly, the link never drew them close.

Lois's daughter Linda, in high school, was like a second mother to her baby half sisters, Laurie and Madelyn, when they arrived. Outspoken Julie was delighted when Charlie presented her with a pony. "I was an instant dad," said Charlie.

But he was also an older dad, with graying hair and a debonair mustache—a man in full, as my wife puts it. Eventually Charlie was lured away from St. Joseph's to become president of the medical staff at Baptist Memorial Hospital. He moved his growing family into a handsome house on a quiet street in Mission Hills, Kansas, a suburb popular with doctors, lawyers, and business executives. There was a hematologist next door, a surgeon across the street, an insurance mogul a few houses away. Charlie's lifelong love of cars had never ended; his circular driveway—where I would eventually see him washing his girlfriend's car with a garden hose and sponge—was often decorated with a low-slung Alpine Sunbeam sports car or, later, a Ford Mustang convertible.

Lois enjoyed tending the gardens. "She was a great cook and a great speaker," Charlie said, and their young daughters made use of the playhouse in the yard. The hovering possessiveness that spoiled his marriage to Jean Landis was gone; if anything, it was Lois who held the reins in their partnership. Charlie said of his formidable wife, "she wasn't dominating, but she held her own." Lois was an active Episcopalian, and she converted Charlie from his father's denomination—Church of Christ—to her own. Together they attended services each Sunday at St. Paul's Church on Main Street.

Charlie loved taking vacations with Lois—just the two of them. No kids. "She was a good golfer and a tremendous fisherman," Charlie remembered. He ended up spending a lot of time around Aspen after all, returning again and again to a cabin on the Fryingpan River near the burgeoning ski resort he had scoffed at years before. The fast-running water with its pools and eddies was a trout hunter's paradise. "I'd sit on a hill above her and say, 'Lois, catch me a fish!' And she would reel one in."

～

"Charlie was a great guy."

This is Jack Moore speaking, Charlie's senior son-in-law. We met over lunch a couple of years after the old man was gone. "He never let anything get to him, and I don't remember ever seeing him really mad. He loved his work but he loved his relaxation, too. He had a sailboat for a while that he took to the lake, and one time he nearly sank it when he forgot to put the plug in the bottom. He had his horses, until the real estate guys talked him into selling his farms."

Jack told me he remembered Charlie for his golf game, which was lethal around the greens, and for the ratty old swim shorts he wore long after they became indecent, and for his loyalty to his mother and sisters, and for the pipe he smoked when he wasn't bumming cigarettes in hospital hallways. "Everybody smoked in hospitals: nurses, doctors, patients," Moore recalled. "Unless you were on oxygen, you smoked."

A quick-witted young man from West Virginia with an interest in caring for animals, Moore attended Kansas State University with plans to be a veterinarian. He changed his mind when an experienced vet told him, "Veterinarians work too hard. You should be an MD." And so Moore pursued medicine while also pursuing the attractive oldest daughter of Lois Grimshaw White. Charlie took Jack under his wing.

It was the 1960s now. Charlie knew, in this age of specialization, that Jack would learn the latest theories and advances in medical school. Charlie wanted to make sure that Jack also learned the basics—the all-around practicality of an old-fashioned general practitioner. He wanted his soon-to-be son-in-law to understand that a doctor doesn't just perform procedures. A doctor cares for people.

"He would get calls at home. I'd be hanging out at his house, and he would ask, 'Would you like to go with me?' Of course I wanted to go," Jack recalled. Any good medical student would jump at a chance to answer emergency calls with the president of a hospital staff.

"But then we'd get there . . .

"I remember a motorcycle accident," Moore recalled. "The patient's face was skinned off. I held it together because I thought the patient was unconscious. But then Charlie spoke to him, and the guy talked back—except his words came out as bubbles on his lips. I had my head between my legs."

Jack was destined to become a talented surgeon, adding many years to the lives of men with prostate cancer. But Charlie connected Jack to the age of unspecialized medicine; he was a link to a time when healers met their patients in every sort of trouble and improvised ways to ease the suffering. "Those guys were really innovative. They were problem solvers," Moore said of Charlie and his generation of mentors.

He gave me this example.

"It was one of those emergency calls. Charlie took me to see a failed suicide at the hospital. The patient had tried to hang himself, and if you've ever seen one, you know a symptom afterward can be a grossly swollen tongue. Well, this poor fellow kept choking on that tongue—aspirating—and the medical team would have to pull the tongue out. This happened over and over until Charlie walked in, sized up the situation, and told the nurse: 'Get me a number two silk.'"

The nurse brought a suture kit. Working quickly, Charlie looped a couple of stitches through the swollen tongue, then stretched the thread to the foot of the bed, where he tied it in a knot. Problem solved. That tongue could not fall back into the throat again.

I thought of the horse tank and Charlie's early open-heart surgeries. Facing a problem, Charlie didn't wait for a perfect solution. He took the next step forward that he could see. Tying a patient's tongue to the foot of his bed never caught on as an emergency medicine technique. But it worked that day, for that patient.

Years later, after Charlie was dead and Jack Moore's great career was done, the son-in-law said this to me: "I don't know anyone who loved medicine as much as Charlie. He went to meetings long after he was a hundred. A group of doctors met over breakfast once a month at seven a.m. Charlie never missed it."

A venerable medical tradition is known as "grand rounds." Students and teaching doctors gather to visit the most interesting cases in a hospital to discuss mysteries and share discoveries. "He attended grand rounds until he couldn't go anymore," Moore said simply.

Loving medicine was not the same as loving trips to the doctor, however. Charlie rarely turned to his colleagues to treat his family. From his early experiences, he had come to believe that most maladies would heal naturally. Those that might not, he preferred to handle himself; forget the specialists. Troubled by a Morton's neuroma in his foot, for example, Charlie settled into his office, injected a nerve-blocking drug into his lower leg and reached for a scalpel. The neuroma, a painful condition in the ball of the foot, is caused by tissue impinging on a nerve. Charlie sliced open his foot, peered inside, and cut away the offending tissue. As he was sewing up his wound, however, an emergency call summoned him to an operating room.

This was a problem. With his numbed and sutured foot, there was no way Charlie could dash to the emergency. Nor could he leave a patient in need. Charlie sent for a wheelchair, and hurriedly wrapped his foot in gauze. Disabled and heroic, he rode to the rescue.

Charlie raised his children with the same light touch he had received from his mother—so light that it almost felt like neglect. His children remember mantras of essential wisdom. Do your best. Do what's right. Keep your daubers up.

That was a new one on me when I first heard it from Charlie's family. They were surprised I had never encountered the expression before: keep your daubers up! Charlie urged elevated daubers at least a hundred, or a thousand, or a million times—so many that the White kids took the expression for granted. When I pressed, no one was 100 percent sure what "daubers" were exactly—only that keeping them up implied determination, equanimity, and a sturdy sort of practical optimism.

I poked around for the meaning, and found that the internet is populated with folks as mystified by the expression as I was. Explanations were widespread, and they fell into two broad categories. One had to do with painting. It seems that the word *daub* is related to the Latin word for white, and that to "daub" originally meant to whitewash or cover up with plaster. So a dauber was a kind of paintbrush used for daubing, and if a person got careless or discouraged and let the dauber drop, the dripping pigment could make a mess.

The other school of internet explainers maintains that the expression derives from hardworking insects known as "mud wasps," or (more relevantly) "mud daubers." While building their nests of layered, plasterlike mud, these industrious little pests keep their noses to their work, their tails high, in that dogged posture that has always represented honest humble labor.

For young people coming of age in the 1960s and 1970s, "keep your daubers up" was a bit stodgy, perhaps. But it's a fine distillation of Charlie's life secrets. It is a Stoic admonition: how we choose to keep our daubers is very much within our power. And the guidance is liberating, creative, in the way that Charlie was free and vibrant. A person gives meaning to the expression by living it. With our daubers up—whatever it means exactly—we're ready for opportunity. We're poised to learn and grow through change. We're alert and alive, determined, unbeaten.

There is readiness in the phrase. Stay sharp. Don't slump. Keep going. Hang in there. Be true to yourself and to your daubers. Ralph Waldo Emerson, a philosopher who knew infinite grief and loss— loss of his father as a boy, loss of his brothers as a youth, loss of his wife as a young lover, loss of a child as a father—kept his daubers up by seeing that *right now* is what matters, because it is the only thing we can touch. The past has slipped beyond our influence and the future is outside our knowing. To be happy and fruitful, we must engage with *right now*.

Conversely, the source of unhappiness and frustration is this, according to Emerson: "Man postpones or remembers, he does not live in the present, but with reverted eyes laments the past, or heedless of the riches that surround him, stands on tiptoe to foresee the future." We "cannot be happy and strong," he concludes, until we live "in the present, above time."

With our daubers up.

Psychologists speak of "flashbulb memories." These are the moments and images that stand out as if floodlit in the dim twilight of our busy, jumbled memories. Jack Moore shared some flashbulb memories of Charlie near the end of his full-time career—though nowhere near the end of his life. There was a party in Jerry Miller's backyard. Miller was an obstetrician-gynecologist with a big personality and lots of friends. Charlie showed up in a grass skirt he had brought home from a trip to Hawaii. While performing the hula on a diving board, Charlie fell into the water and was nearly dragged to the bottom by the weight of his wet skirt.

Another flashbulb: Charlie had a dachshund he loved very much. The extent of his love was untested, though, until the dog was crushed under a falling tree limb during a wild Kansas windstorm. Back broken, the dog was paralyzed in its hind legs, but Charlie could not bring himself to put the animal down. So Moore remembered a low-slung dog strapped to a roller skate, dragging himself happily through Charlie's house, trailed by the odor of his uncontrolled bowels.

Moore remembered Charlie at the center of roving celebrations up and down the street, singing at the top of his lungs.

He remembered Charlie steering his latest stylish car into the very best parking spaces outside University of Missouri football games—relying on his license plate, stamped MD, to justify his presence.

He remembered a birthday card Charlie sent him shortly after the introduction of the blockbuster drug Viagra. On the cover of the card was a photo of the little blue pill next to a picture of a rooster. The message inside: "Rise and Shine!"

Into this light and happy period of Charlie's long life came another season of pain. Lois was diagnosed with cancer and, as Moore and others remember it, she accepted her fate as inevitable—perhaps before it really was. "Psychologically, it wiped her out," said Moore, whose own medical specialty put him in daily contact with cancer. "She let herself get weaker and weaker. Charlie couldn't understand why she didn't fight harder. He felt she gave up."

I remembered Charlie's rather skeptical view of medicine—which seemed strange coming from a doctor. When people close to him got sick, he treated them with bed rest and plenty of water. Charlie urged faith in the ability to thrive.

Lois seemed to lack faith.

Another of Moore's flashbulb memories: Lois was upstairs in bed, with a bell at her bedside to ring in time of need.

The bell jingled.

Though nearly ninety, Charlie jumped up and darted upstairs, then came down trudging. "She didn't need anything," he reported.

I suspect Lois did need something. Maybe she needed to know that someone cared enough to come running. Maybe she needed to feel that she would not die alone. She may have needed a sense of agency, of power—this woman who, before she was sick, dominated every room she walked into with her combination of beauty and confidence. The valley of death is perhaps the most difficult place for a Stoic self-confidence to survive. There we come face-to-face with the ultimate limit of our power, the humbling fact that no creature has ever been able to change.

I can't condemn Lois's choice to embrace her fate rather than fight it. Fate would be fulfilled regardless. I don't scorn the tests she set for Charlie to jump up and run the stairs when she felt lonely or scared. Nor—as far as I ever learned—did Charlie. He outlived Lois by almost twenty years. The exasperation vanished. The edges of the pain wore down and softened. He never told me about a jangling bell.

All he ever told me about Lois—the memories he cherished— were stories of her loveliness and strength.

ten

Our story began on that blast-furnace Sunday morning when I looked across the street and saw Charlie with his garden hose and sponge. Lois had been dead about a dozen years. A very long life is like a very large mansion. There are many rooms and all the rooms are big. Charlie had not one but two careers as a doctor: years as a general practitioner, followed by decades as an anesthesiologist. His retirement was as long as most careers. He had not one but two long marriages, plus years as a single man. The train station he saw rising from the dirt as a boy had a long heyday and fell into disrepair, languished as an old white elephant until the city almost gave up on it, then was restored in homage to Kansas City's history—all in the confines of the mansion of Charlie's life.

He didn't lose a step in his nineties. Besides his regular meeting of physicians to keep up on the latest medical advances and his appearances at the hospital for grand rounds, Charlie also faithfully attended meetings of his Investment Club, a group of younger men (the whole world was younger now) who researched stocks and rode the bull market before the dot-com bubble burst—then kept going. Charlie twice traveled to Haiti with his friend, pediatrician Herb Davis, to give checkups and administer vaccines to impoverished children. His work had come full circle then, from the boyhood dinner table where he listened admiringly to the stories of medical missionaries and decided to be a doctor, to these missions of his own. Just as he was during the Depression, Charlie was a general practitioner again in Haiti, diagnosing every variety of ailment and offering practical solutions for patients in desperate straits. Charlie often said that being a doctor wasn't a job or even a profession. It was a privilege: for no other employment brought a person into such intimate positions of trust with others. On his second trip to Haiti, Charlie was ninety-nine years old.

In Haiti or at home, everywhere Charlie went he was asked for his secret of longevity. His answer was deflating. It was just luck, he said. His genome, over which he had no influence, had not betrayed him with a weak heart or a wasting disease. Unlike his father, Charlie never saw his number come up in the cosmic lottery of freak accidents. Some people get lung cancer having never smoked at all. Charlie smoked for decades without doing any meaningful damage.

Luck.

His stepdaughter Linda began feeling poorly after a vacation at age sixty-six. A scan disclosed tumors throughout her body and she was gone within months. A few weeks after she died, Charlie turned 102.

Luck.

Charlie accepted his fortune and lived in the moment. On his ninety-fifth birthday, he entertained a crowd of friends by peeling off his jacket and jamming with the band on his saxophone. At a time when most of his contemporaries were long dead, Charlie struck up a grand new romance. He became the beau of one of Kansas City's most glamorous widows, a vivacious transplant from Texas some twenty years younger named Mary Ann Walton Cooper. "A damn knockout," is how Jack Moore described her, and I have to agree, having met her for the first time not long after I saw Charlie washing her car.

She was as vibrant as she was beautiful. I knew her for roughly four minutes before she regaled me with a story from the days when her late husband, a surgeon, relied on Charlie to handle his anesthesia. Mary Ann herself had needed a surgery and her husband assembled a team to perform it. After Charlie put her under, the doctors bared her torso for the operation. She had written in lipstick across her breast: "Do Not Open Until Christmas."

Mary Ann set her sights on Charlie not long after he was widowed—for a simple reason, she told me. They made each other laugh, and she knew they would have a lot of fun together. Her previous boyfriend, ninety-one at the time, was philosophical when she broke the news that she would be the steady girl of ninety-two-year-old Charlie. "I just got beat out by an older man," he said.

And fun they had. For years they were weekend regulars at the Blue Hills Country Club dining room. Mary Ann would drive over from her house for a predinner cocktail in Charlie's den. Sometimes when her car appeared I couldn't help knocking on the door to say hello. Between the two of them, they filled each visit with a jolt of the life force that Chinese philosophers call *ch'i*. It has to do with vigor and morale and it flows from a right relationship to the order of things.

Charlie and Mary Ann channeled *ch'i*. They understood that sorrow requires no pursuit; it finds us whenever it chooses. It had found them before. It would find them again. But when pain was hunting elsewhere, they resolved to enjoy the gifts of each day. Laughter was one of those gifts. One example: Mary Ann laughed hardest when Charlie scolded the rector at his church for announcing his one hundredth birthday during Sunday services. "The ladies will think I am too old to date," he complained.

Mary Ann and Charlie took a disappointed look across the street at our family. Oh, they liked us well enough, but they were convinced that my wife and I should lighten up. One Friday evening when I dropped by before they went out to dinner, I happened to mention the busy weekend my family had in store, full of soccer games, birthday parties, and other child-centered activities.

"Oh, no, dear!" Mary Ann scolded me, slightly wrinkling her perfectly accentuated lips. (She was a genius of lipstick.) "You go tell your wife to get dressed up because the two of you are going out—with no children! They'll be *fine* without you."

Charlie nodded as she continued. "The marriage *always* comes first," she said. "Your children will grow up and leave. They live their lives and you must live yours. Why, when my boys were young, I never let five o'clock arrive without freshening my makeup and getting my husband's drink ready."

My wife rolled her eyes when I returned home and shared this advice. She may have said something to the effect of, "Fix your own damn drink." But I wasn't one to argue with Mary Ann Cooper about life—she was a blast of vitality—or about parenting. She was, I had learned, mother to the actor Chris Cooper, who as a boy did whatever he did while his mother perfected her makeup and tended the family bar. Not long before I met her, she was the guest of honor—with Charlie on her arm—at a party to watch on television as her son received an Academy Award.

This fine romance of Charlie White and Mary Ann Cooper endured as long as Charlie lived. As Mary Ann entered her late eighties and Charlie reached his last years, her incandescence began to dim. Her memory left her, but Charlie never did. He sat beside her holding her hand, sometimes in quiet communion, sometimes speaking or singing to her softly.

In those last years, I would realize that a month or two or even a season had passed without a visit to Charlie. Each morning, I carried his newspaper up the driveway and propped it by his door to let him know I was thinking of him. But I squandered time I should have spent with him. Only an idiot, or the father of teens, would fail to spend time with a friend who is 103 . . . 104 . . . 105 . . . But then I would pay a call and all would be forgiven, because Charlie was sailing along undaunted.

He was 106 when I had an idea to write an essay about the brief career of young Walt Disney as an animator in Kansas City. I had done a little reading and came to the realization that nearly all of American animation until about 1975—all the cartoons I grew up on—could be traced through a family tree of artists to the handful of young men Disney recruited to his failed Kansas City studio fifty years earlier. This was a chain reaction of creativity, like Florence during the Renaissance or Silicon Valley in the late twentieth century.

Charlie had not known Walt Disney, but they shared sidewalks. I rang Charlie's doorbell and asked him to tell me about Kansas City in 1921. We sat in his kitchen and, without missing a beat, he opened the time machine of his memory and ushered me inside.

A century after he climbed down from the train in the Kansas City stockyards, Charlie's memory was extraordinary. He recalled the names of all the movie theaters in town, and not just the names but the street addresses. I thought I knew where the Newman Theater had stood, that vast auditorium where Disney's shorts were first projected and radio met Carleton Coon and Joe Sanders. But I had the wrong corner; Charlie corrected me. He walked me along the flowered paths and under the bewitching lights of long-ago Electric Park. He erased the decay from the neighborhood where Disney had his little studio above a diner and kept a pet mouse in his desk drawer—the mouse that would inspire one of history's most famous artistic creations.

Interspersed among these details were leaps and digressions and asides that played across the decades: commentary on a recent news event I had covered, questions about my family, small talk about lawn maintenance. Somehow his mind was keen and supple in the past and in the present. He remained as interested in tomorrow as in yesterday.

The vitality of Charlie's mind planted a dream in mine—a fantasy, really. Recalling our first conversation, as Charlie was leaning on his pitching wedge and lamenting his inability to play golf, I began thinking that it would make one heck of a story to get the old man out on the links one last time. How many 106-year-old golfers could there be in the world?

I mentioned my idea to Charlie, who smiled but shook his head. He knew, even if I didn't, that time finally was catching up to Charlie White.

He slipped on a patch of ice outside his front door one frigid day, and his ankle broke with a pop. I believe this was the winter of his 106th ride around the sun. When I heard the news from his son-in-law Doug, I thought, *Maybe this is the beginning of the end*. But then I stopped by the assisted living facility where Charlie was recuperating and found him in grand spirits, holding court for a steady stream of visitors. Herb Davis, the organizer of the trips to Haiti, stopped by just as a staff member wheeled a cart into the room with a box of wine and some glasses on top. "It's happy hour!" she announced, and we gave a little toast to Charlie's health. It must have worked, because he was soon back at home and attending his round of weekly clubs and meetings.

Months went by before Doug reported the next health emergency. Charlie was experiencing hallucinations. Not just flashes of light or patterns in front of his eyes—but strange and colorful creatures that appeared to have made themselves at home in his den. His doctors weren't sure what to make of this. It could mean the onset of dementia. It could be a sign of a brain tumor. Whatever it was, it didn't seem good.

As it happened, a friend of mine had written an essay a few years earlier about his elderly father's hallucinations. From that, I learned about a syndrome that was no more ominous than simple failing eyesight. The brain is working just fine—in fact, it's working overtime to fill the frame of vision even when the eyes are no longer providing enough data. The brain invents things.

This seemed like a possible diagnosis. The most dangerous aspect of this affliction, my friend had written, was that patients might be frightened by their visions or fearful of losing their minds. So I crossed the street to size up Charlie's mood.

"It's the strangest thing," he told me when we settled into his den. "I see these people and animals and things as clearly as I see you right now. More clearly."

"There!" he said, pointing at the chest where he displayed his antique duelling pistols. Souvenirs of his adventures in Peru, the old guns had long outlasted the little monkey named Bill Duncan. "Do you see that?"

Before I could reply, Charlie answered for me. "No, of course you don't. You don't see it, because it isn't there."

I shared what little I knew about Charles Bonnet syndrome. It was named for an eighteenth-century scientist who described the condition when it struck his elderly grandfather, who—like Charlie—was sharp as a tack but nearly blind. The affliction calls up different visions in different people, but generally the visions are benign. Some sufferers see cartoonlike figures. I read about a man who saw cows grazing on his living room carpet. My writer-friend's father once mentioned that the road was lined with signs in Hebrew.

"What do they say?" my friend asked.

"You know I can't read Hebrew," his father replied.

Charlie nodded amiably as I reported this. He had worried about the hallucinations when they started, but now they didn't seem so bad, he said. There were much worse things that could happen to a person. He knew, because some had happened to him.

So he shrugged off the broken ankle and was unfazed by the hallucinations. I was sure the end was coming, though, when—at age 107—Charlie was hospitalized with pneumonia.

One of the early giants of modern medicine, William Osler, commented on the high fatality rate for geriatric pneumonia cases in his 1892 textbook, *The Principles and Practice of Medicine*. Osler wrote: "It has been termed the natural end of the old man." In fact, the disease is so efficient at bringing lives to relatively merciful ends that it has a nickname: the old man's friend.

Charlie was an old man if anyone was. I didn't want to lose my friend, but I was glad that a comfortable ride had pulled up alongside him to carry him home. In this philosophical mood, I asked for his hospital room number and went to say good-bye.

He was in a large private room on a high floor of a hospital near the Plaza. *Professional courtesy*, I thought to myself. The shades were down at midday, casting a twilight gloaming over the scene. Charlie's thin frame slumbered beneath a white sheet. The only sounds were his light snore, almost like a baby's, and the beep of the heart monitor with each jagged leap of the green-lit display. I froze in the doorway, then crept backward into the hall.

A nurse found me standing there a few minutes later.

"May I help you?"

"I was going to visit Dr. White," I said, "but he's sleeping."

"Oh," she said. "Go on in. We're about to wake him anyway."

So I sidled to Charlie's bedside and stood a moment, still unsure. His steady breathing broke in a snort; he jolted; his eyes opened and he said, "Who's there?"

I announced myself, and apologized for waking him, but Charlie's eyes fastened on me and he immediately launched into a conversation. I had tiptoed to his bedside as if into a tomb. Instead we were friends who easily picked up our loose ends.

Charlie assured me he was feeling quite well after a few bags of IV fluids and antibiotics. We chatted for a while, and it was the same as always. Charlie gave me a history of pneumonia treatment, admonishing me to remember that Osler wrote in the days before penicillin. He told me how the hospital he occupied had come to be, recalling each building, wing, and annex as it had risen. He asked after my family and counseled me to trust that my children would turn out fine. He was as lively as usual, and I quickly concluded that Charlie had slipped the Grim Reaper again.

This was confirmed when a white-jacketed cardiologist came into the room. It was my friend Matt from the neighborhood, a former collegiate swimmer at Yale. Charlie was in good hands. Matt double-checked a few test results on his clipboard and pronounced himself thoroughly satisfied with his patient's recovery. Charlie would be discharged within a day, he said.

"You might want to make a note of this, Matt," I suggested. "You probably won't discharge many one-hundred-and-seven-year-old pneumonia patients in your career."

And still, he had one ace up his sleeve.

At 108, Charlie at last lost his independence. Even with help from Madelyn and Doug, he could no longer live at home. He moved into a fancy nursing home where he could share the lobby with Mary Ann, holding her hand.

Doug told me one day that Charlie was fading fast. For the first time, the forever man was telling his loved ones that death was near, and assuring them that he was ready. Charlie's wide circle of friends and admirers braced for fate to catch at his collar. But springtime blossomed again in the Missouri River valley, and the trees spread their green umbrellas for summer. Charlie had a change of heart. His birthday was near, and having come so far, he decided that he might as well keep going to 109.

How unlike Charlie, I thought to myself, to imagine that he had control over something as powerful and capricious as death. One of the core teachings of Stoicism is that death keeps its own datebook; it can come at any time, and the only certainty is that it will eventually get to you. Therefore, "let us postpone nothing," in the words of the amiable Roman philosopher and playwright Seneca. "Let us balance life's books every day." That had been Charlie's approach for a lifetime. But now he set his course for 109 and delayed his final accounting.

The glories of May warmed into June, sweltered into July. One long, hot day followed another until the day came when my phone rang and Doug told me that Charlie was gone. I had lost track of the days, quite honestly. I checked a calendar—then shook my head, which was swimming lightly in a flood of amazement and delight. Feelings I often associated with Charlie. It was August 17, 2014.

Quietly, in the wee hours after his birthday, he let go.

Hundreds of people gathered for Charlie's funeral. Our four kids spent the twenty-minute ride to St. Paul's Episcopal Church each absorbed in a vast digital universe on a personal screen. We pulled up to the entrance, and the door of the family van slid open as if by magic. We left the climate control of our vehicle for the climate control of the church. Overhead, so far up as to be invisible, aluminum tubes carried thousands of passengers across the continent at hundreds of miles per hour. What began among the horses and wagons and slow-moving trains of Galesburg, Illinois, more than a century earlier, came to its close in a world transformed.

The sanctuary was pillars of stone and windows of glowing glass, built by the people of a young city to make them feel like they'd been there forever. Old as the church felt, it was younger than Charlie. With more laughter than tears, and more music than mourning, we said good-bye.

"I haven't given it much thought," Charlie once told an interviewer who asked for his philosophy of life. Many a curious writer and oral historian paid calls on Charlie during his final decade. He shared his stories with newspaper and television and magazine reporters. Everyone was charmed as I was.

This particular interviewer posed what seemed like an obvious question. Charlie had a century to think about it. Wondering over the meaning of life must have started the day that his father was snatched by ruthless fate. Yet the question seemed to catch him off guard.

"I just plowed along," he finally said. In fact, Charlie had adopted his mother's philosophy, which was "so simple," and served Charlie so well: "Do the right thing." This was a very practical philosophy, he continued. "If you do the right thing, it covers a whole raft of situations."

Warming to the question, Charlie went on. "I always say: This will pass." Whatever the challenge, "you've got to work through it, and hold the line, and don't fall apart. Stick in there. There's no future in negativism."

And finally: "Nobody's going to do it for you. You've got to do your own paddling. So always keep your daubers up—no matter what."

Could it be that this life, in this tempest of change, through economic depression and prosperity, in wartime and peacetime, youth and age, joy and grief, boiled down to such simplicity?

Among Charlie's things after he was gone, his family found a single sheet of notepaper with a heading that said "Claridge Court." This was the community where he spent his last days.

The interviewer's question had stayed with him. As he felt his life ending, Charlie sat with the notepad and distilled his philosophy of life. He filled the sheet of paper front and back in flowing ballpoint pen. Charlie was a man of action. He wrote in definitive commands.

Think freely.

That's where he started, boldly.

Practice patience.

Smile often.

Savor special moments.

Charlie's list poured onto the page. The lettering was even and orderly, with no words scratched out and no apparent hesitation. No statement was more than a few words long—as though the operating system of a happy and productive life could be written in thirty or forty crisp lines of code. Make and keep friends. Tell loved ones how you feel. Forgive and seek forgiveness.

Feel deeply.

Observe miracles.

Make them happen.

He wrote about trusting yourself enough to take risks. About opening yourself to opportunity and being ready to seize it. About finding beauty in the world: the thrumming rain, the ephemeral rainbow, the glow of sunrise.

Be soft sometimes.

Cry when you need to.

Make some mistakes.

Learn from them.

As I studied Charlie's list—his active steps to a fulfilling life—it seemed to me that each one, by itself, was like a greeting card or a Facebook meme. Charlie's takeaway lessons from more than a century of living were things we already know, for we have heard them a thousand times.

But after a few years to think about it—years in which, like the poet T. S. Eliot, "I have seen the eternal footman hold my coat and snicker"—I have arrived at a theory that a life well led consists of two parts. In the first part, we are complexifiers. We take the simple world of childhood and discover its complications. Nothing is quite as it seems. Things are not as we were told. We say, "yes—but . . ." and "on the other hand . . ." and "maybe it's not that easy."

Then, if we live long enough, we might soften into the second stage, and become simplifiers. For all the books on all the shelves of all the world's libraries, life must in the end be lived as a series of discrete moments and individual decisions. What we face may be complicated, but what we do about it is simple. "Do the right thing," Laura White told her son. "Do unto others," a teacher told his disciples, "as you would have them do unto you."

Charlie lived so long that the veil of complexity fell away entirely and he saw that life is not so hard as we tend to make it. Or rather:

no matter how hard life may be, the way we ought to live becomes a distillate of few words. The essentials are familiar not because they are trite, but because they are true.

I picture him even now, his eyes dimmed but his mind bright as a diamond, filling this sheet of paper with his simple truths.

Work hard.

Spread joy.

Take a chance.

Enjoy wonder.

And I have my answer, my book for my kids. How does one thrive through a maelstrom of change? By standing on ground that is permanent.

Acknowledgments

We chose our home in Kansas in 2007 for two reasons: it had a bedroom for each of our four children, and the school bus stopped at our driveway. Discovering Charlie White across the street was pure luck. And yet, the unknown jackpot of our new address was the World's Best Next-Door Neighbor. Doug Dalgleish—Mister D to the Von Drehle kids and son-in-law to Charlie White—became a second, far more delightful, dad to our children, while connecting me to an expanding universe of extraordinary friends.

The rest of Charlie's family has also been generous and supportive of this book, starting with Madelyn White Dalgleish—Charlie's youngest daughter—and her sister Laurie White. Another of Charlie's sons-in-law, Jack Moore, was free with his memories of the old man (and with medical advice when I needed it). Charlie's stepson Bill Grimshaw and Bill's daughter Lois Grimshaw shared their memories and mementoes. Indeed, everyone in Charlie's circle of family and friends answered without stinting when we asked for help.

An oral history recorded by the professionals at Voices in Time was an invaluable resource. They caught Charlie's charming voice and favorite stories exactly as I remembered them, and their recordings helped me to sort out a few points of confusion after Charlie was no longer around to help me.

This little book was a long time coming. If I listed all the people who picked me up, shared my load, lightened my days, and warmed me with kindness along the way, a slim volume would turn into a thick one. *Observe miracles*, Charlie advised, and I have followed his counsel while pondering the miracle of love and concern with which friends and family have surrounded me. (My friend John Herron, a professional historian of Kansas City and beyond, was kind enough to read behind me and mop up some mistakes.)

I am so grateful to Henry, Ella, Addie, and Clara—those kids with whom I read so many books long ago. Thank you for your patience: you make me joyful even when I don't show it. Karen Ball has been my inspiration and the best teammate a writer could have, responsible for discovering many of the best things in this book.

Thank you to Esther Newberg and her team at ICM Partners; to supportive bosses at the *Washington Post* and *Time* magazine, among them Nancy Gibbs, Michael Duffy, Ruth Marcus, and the late, great Fred Hiatt; to Jonathan Karp, Hana Park, Jackie Seow, and the gang at Simon & Schuster.

And finally, chief among that gang: Priscilla Painton, who set this tale in motion by giving me a dream job when she hired me at *Time*. She picked up Charlie's story after she became a shepherd of books. This gifted editor is something more: an exquisite human being.

About the Author

DAVID VON DREHLE is an opinion columnist for the *Washington Post*, a prize-winning magazine writer, and the author of several books. He lives in suburban Kansas City with his wife, journalist Karen Ball.